# SHAMANIC
# REIKI

*Expanded Ways of Working with*
*Universal Life Force Energy*

First published by O-Books, 2008
Reprinted, 2010
O-Books is an imprint of John Hunt Publishing Ltd., Laurel House, Station Approach,
Alresford, Hants, SO24 9JH, UK
office1@o-books.net
www.o-books.com

For distributor details and how to order please visit the 'Ordering' section on our website.

ISBN: 978 1 84694 037 8

A CIP catalogue record for this book is available from the British Library.

Design: Stuart Davies

Printed and bound by CPI Group (UK) Ltd, Croydon, CR0 4YY

We operate a distinctive and ethical publishing philosophy in all
areas of our business, from our global network of authors to
production and worldwide distribution.

# SHAMANIC
# REIKI

*Expanded Ways of Working with*
*Universal Life Force Energy*

Llyn Roberts and Robert Levy

BOOKS

Winchester, UK
Washington, USA

# CONTENTS

# ENDORSEMENTS

"Students often ask me if Reiki and shamanic healing can be bridged together. Llyn Roberts and Robert Levy brilliantly teach all of us that yes they can and more importantly show us how. There is a great need for *Shamanic Reiki*. This book teaches us about the power of love, light, and respect for all of life. Roberts and Levy did a magnificent job."
**Sandra Ingerman**, Author of *Soul Retrieval* and *How to Heal Toxic Thoughts.*

"No ordinary book, *Shamanic Reiki* introduces the combination of Reiki and shamanism with rare empathy, wisdom and insight. This is a book that touches the heart of the human condition."
**Ipupiara Makunaiman**, Brazilian Amazonian shaman and healer of the Ure-reu-wau-wau tribe, the "People from the Stars."

"The alchemy of shamanism and Reiki is nothing less than pure gold in the hands of Llyn Roberts and Robert Levy. *Shamanic Reiki* brings the concept of energy healing to a whole new level. More than a how-to-book, it speaks to the health of the human spirit, a journey we must all complete."
**Brian Luke Seaward, Ph.D.**, Author of *Stand Like Mountain, Flow Like Water* and *Quiet Mind, Fearless Heart.*

"*Shamanic Reiki* offers the gift of healing magic. A practical, relevant book with a depth that speaks to the soul, this is a vital reference for both shamanic and Reiki practitioners. Roberts and Levy provide all the skills needed to heal ourselves and others, and to know our souls more deeply. Fascinating reading for anyone interested in health and well being, with knowledge that can easily be put to good use in everyday life. This is one to keep and refer to often."
**Ross Heaven**, Author of *Love's Simple Truths*, *The Way of the Lover* and *Plant Spirit Shamanism.*

"Shamanic healing techniques are helpful in removing obstacles on ones spiritual path. In the same way, they can help to remove similar energy blocks which create illness. The understanding of energy as a healing and wholing tool, described in great detail by the authors, will help the Reiki practitioner understand some of the phenomena which can occur during (and as a result of) Reiki treatments. *Shamanic Reiki* is a wonderful, easy to follow instruction guide which illuminates the matrix behind shamanic and energetic healing. All praise to Llyn and Robert for their fine work."

**Paula Horan**, Author of *Exploring Reiki, 108 Questions and Answers.*

"Finally we have an inspiring book that weaves together two important models of healing – shamanism and Reiki. Roberts and Levy demonstrate clearly and gracefully from their own extensive practice how vital it is for everyone, whether client or healer, to be worthy channels and vessels of the Life Force. The authors are reliable and sensible guides who lead us gently into a deeper understanding of the dynamics of health and wellbeing."

**Tom Cowan**, Author of *Yearning for the Wind, Fire in the Head: Shamanism and the Celtic Spirit, Shamanism as a Spiritual Practice for Daily Life* and *The Way of the Saints: Prayers, Practices, and Meditation.*

"I have been healed by great shamans from many cultures and by great Reiki masters. I have felt the magical power of the two combined through personal healings from Llyn Roberts. Now, this incredible book, *Shamanic Reiki*, opens the door for all of us. Llyn and Robert guide us on a journey into healing and self-discovery that integrates ancient techniques with the needs of our modern world."

**John M. Perkins**, New York Times best selling author of *Confessions of An Economic Hit Man, Shapeshifting* and *The World Is As You Dream It.*

"*Shamanic Reiki* is a magnificent book. It honors and blends the timeless wisdom of ancient healing traditions with emerging new approaches and practical teachings. It is a rainbow bridge between worlds, honoring the best of these worlds. The concept that shamanic ancient healing energy is

similar to Reiki opens a new horizon combining the riches of both healing traditions. These teachings provide us with clues for how to participate with living earth wisdom."
**Cleicha Toscano**, Peruvian born shaman, healer and elder.

"*Shamanic Reiki* opens a valuable toolbox for those seeking to expand their traditional Reiki practice. Roberts and Levy offer a generous array of approaches, encouraging the reader to choose what works best for them according to their unique relationship to spirit and whatever's called for in the midst of healing. *Shamanic Reiki* gave me a lot of ideas for my own practice and variations to familiar techniques that I hope to explore."
**Christopher Penczak**, Author of *Magick of Reiki*.

# ACKNOWLEDGEMENTS

## ROBERT LEVY

In the summer of 1995, I took my first steps on a healing path that began with studying shamanism and quickly led to being attuned to Reiki. Since this time, I have worked with many teachers whom I wish to acknowledge. Without their guidance, I would still be a struggling novice.

I believe that both shamanism and Reiki are not static modalities, but are constantly adapting to the time and location of the practitioner. Each person who becomes a shamanic or Reiki teacher brings his or her own slant and individual flavorings to the practice. Each shamanic student should, in my opinion, take what resonates for them and adapt it to their uniqueness. That is what I have done. What I have learned from both western and indigenous shamans has been molded to my own personality and whatever spirit was guiding, as it was placed into my *healing basket*.

Because shamanic topics are typically taught in both similar yet different ways, it is impossible for me to remember the sources for everything I have contributed to this book. Therefore, I apologize for not being more specific about who taught me what. I also acknowledge that sprit herself has been my most powerful teacher, weaving, adapting and integrating what was received from my human teachers.

I therefore wish to acknowledge the following people who have guided, pushed and otherwise kept me on a healing path that began long ago: Tom Cowan, Christina Pratt, Nan Moss, David Corbin, John Matthews, Alberto Villoldo, Michael Harner, Robert Moss, Hank Wasselman and Hanakia Zedec. I also wish to thank Reiki masters Enoch Davis, Steven Scheld and Raja Shaheen, plus all the past, present and future members of the New York Shamanic Circle.

I offer special thanks to the following people, who afforded me the respect of a *colleague* long before I reached that stage, and beyond being my teachers, have also become good friends: Llyn Roberts, John Perkins, Dr. Eve Bruce and Aimee Morgana.

I thank Llyn Roberts, my co-author, for harmoniously working with me to put the work we both love into words, and for her love, kindness and patience.

My deepest gratitude goes to Ipupiara Makunaiman and Cleicha Toscano, whose final push anchored me fully onto the path of being a healer. They helped me realize that despite not being an indigenous shaman, what spirit whispers into my own ears (and has since 1995), is just as valid as what spirit is whispering into their ears. Ipu and Cleicha's love, guidance and confidence in me helped open my heart so I could hear and trust spirit's voice. Because of this, I recognize spirit as the ultimate and only source of healing and power. For this, I am eternally grateful.

And finally, to Shigeko LaPlaca, for no reason other than I love her!

Robert Levy, New York City and North Miami, FL
July 2007


## SPECIAL ACKNOWLEDGEMENTS

Llyn Roberts and Robert Levy extend special thanks to the following people for their invaluable contributions during the editing process of *Shamanic Reiki*:

Bob Southard: Shamanic Reiki master practitioner and hypnotherapist. Bob developed the Hypnojourney™ technique and is the author of *Ordinary Secrets ~ Notes for Your Spiritual Journey*. Bob also co-produced the *Pathways to Inner Peace* CD series (meditations, journeys and Hypnojourney™) with Llyn Roberts. Bob has worked with Dream Change for many years and sits on its board of directors. For more information about Bob and his work: www.dreamchange.org and www.boston-mystery.com

Mary Warejcka: Shamanic Reiki master teacher and practitioner offering individual sessions and classes in the Dallas, TX area. A professional writer and editor, Mary also holds a master's degree in Theological Studies, focusing on helping people connect with their inner wisdom, others, spirit and the elements. Mary can be reached at 214-929-7902, or mary@manypathsway.net Website: www.manypathsway.net

Susan Dowling-Slover: Shamanic and Energy Medicine practitioner. A graduate of the Barbara Brennan School of Healing, Susan has studied with eminent shamans worldwide. She fosters ceremonial shamanic and earth-honoring traditions as practices of daily living, mentors healers and shamanic practitioners and maintains a private practice in Connecticut with adults and children. Su may be reached at The Shoreline Center for Wholistic Health 203-453-5520 or at www.thepeacehouse.net and su@thepeacehouse.net

## AUTHORS' NOTE

Disclaimers can minimize the potentials of spiritual/energetic intervention and undermine the practical intelligence of its practitioners. That said, this book is offered for informational purposes, its user accepting all responsibility for applying the information presented. Energy healing systems such as shamanism, Reiki and Shamanic Reiki are commonly considered as complimentary therapies to medical or psychological modalities and spiritual practitioners aren't sanctioned to diagnose or treat medical or psychological illnesses. In such cases, clients and practitioners are advised to contact a licensed holistic professional.

**DEDICATION**

To all who are ready to step through the Shamanic Reiki portal ~
May you transform, and in doing so, transform our world.


To the Universal Life Force Energy
Who knows what's good for us even when we ourselves don't, yet
shows infinite patience as we wake up to our own wisdom.

# CHAPTER ONE

# REIKI, SHAMANISM AND

# SHAMANIC REIKI

Many believe that in the far distant past of the universe was the void. They believe that no intelligent life manifested to give distinction to this void. Neither time nor matter existed. Then something happened. From this void a universe spawned. Eventually, within that universe, our galaxy, our sun, our planet, and the species that lived and do now live on it also spawned.

Of the many issues surrounding the myth of creation, we'll discuss one. Many believe that creation wasn't a random act of related happenings that suddenly resulted in a universe. Instead, they conceive that we and everything in the universe are here because of the wish of a higher consciousness. Why, how or when it happened doesn't concern them. They only know that this higher power, which we'll call spirit, is responsible. This belief is based on one word, faith.

Faith is defined in part as a belief and complete trust in something for which there is no proof. To paraphrase a line from *Miracle on 34$^{th}$ Street*, "Faith is our believing in something when common sense tells us not to."

This book is about the hands-on healing modality called Reiki and so much more. It will show you how to integrate shamanic and other approaches into a Reiki session to deepen your practice and empower your client. We'll show you how the progression from Reiki to shamanic work is a natural one because they're based on similar principles. Questions relating to where Reiki energy comes from or why shamanism actually works won't be discussed. We really don't know and think it's unlikely that anyone else does either. What we share in this book must be taken on the same kind of faith that supports a belief in spirit, but which can then only be proven through experience. Don't blindly accept what you read, but do please journey through these pages with an engaged heart and mind. Open to the possibility that healing can be ecstatic, enriching your life in ways you never dreamed possible. Dream big and let your experience guide you.

## Reiki Basics

Reiki was re-discovered by Dr Mikao Usui in the early 1900s, and its beginnings are shrouded in controversy. Its legacy was passed on verbally and experientially and written down later. Although it may be in vogue to argue who said or did what, or what is or isn't the proper way to practice Reiki, we won't deal with these controversies. There are enough books on the shelves dissecting Reiki as if it were a turkey ready to be carved and presented on a platter. Although some get embroiled in arguments of the intellect, the important thing is to practice Reiki in a way that's harmonious for you.

Working with Reiki is working with energy. It's simple, safe and easy. The word Reiki comes from the Japanese and is generally translated as "universal life force energy." Practicing it means becoming a channel to allow the universal energy to pass through you so it can be received by another. What sets Reiki apart from other hands-on healing modalities is that to become a channel to receive the energy you must be attuned by a Reiki master. The attunement opens you to receive and channel Reiki energy to others.

An analogy would be to imagine that deep within you is an AM radio receiver making it possible to accept, perceive and experience everything that's powered by AM radio frequencies. Assume that everything in our normal world is on those AM frequencies. Imagine the Reiki energy however, is fueled by FM frequency. Therefore, to receive the Reiki energy, you'd also need an FM receiver. The attunement process would be similar to implanting that FM receiver into your body. You would now perceive and experience from FM as well as AM, enabling you to accept the Reiki energy and channel it to others.

Reiki masters teach and attune people to Reiki, which is generally divided into three levels. People all over the world attending Level One workshops learn about the history of Reiki, the attunement process and receive attunement(s). One Reiki school divides the attunements into four sections and others combine them into one. Yet still others may divide the attunement altogether differently. If done with the intent of performing attunements for Level One students, all of these attunements are valid. Practicing and experiencing Reiki is usually included in the first workshop.

Level Two workshops intensify the Reiki energy, allow the practitioner to channel energy at a distance and to effect deeper healing. Level Two also introduces the symbols that empower these intentions: the Power Symbol, the Mental Emotional Symbol and the Long Distance Healing Symbol. Each symbol is explained and the students practice the use of those symbols.

Level Three opens you to channel greater degrees of Reiki energy than Level Two, and students receive an additional master symbol(s). They are empowered to perform attunements and teach their own Reiki levels. Those attuned to the third level of Reiki are called Reiki masters. The approaches vary widely as some teach Level Three in a weekend workshop while others tutor aspiring teachers in apprenticeships spanning months or years. A variant to the Level Three teacher training is the Level Three master-practitioner level. These are typically weekend workshops empowering master-level energy for serious practitioners not inspired to teach, or in preparation for the teacher level. Reiki master-practitioners do not teach Reiki and they do not pass attunements.

The term master in association with Reiki can put some people off. This may be in part because the word master has been typically applied to a craft. Long ago, if a young boy wished to be a carpenter, he began work as an apprentice. After becoming proficient at the craft over a period of time, the lad was no longer an apprentice but a journeyman. This meant that he knew more than an apprentice, but was not skilled enough to be called a craftsman. More time would pass and as the young man's skill increased, he left the title journeyman behind and became a craftsman, a carpenter. But as he grew in experience and talent, the seasoned man who was once the boy apprentice would be called a master carpenter, master craftsman. In this context, master implies excellence and knowledge beyond the common practitioner in any given craft. The same might be true for religious disciples demonstrating high levels of spiritual mastery. Using this context the same should be true for Reiki, yet this is rarely the case.

Although some schools require practitioners to show a level of knowledge and expertise that satisfies their teachers before they apply the title Reiki master, most do not. It helps to think of the term Reiki master as implying less about the individual and more about the energy itself. All attunements and Reiki sessions are valid and powerful. Becoming a Reiki master means that a person can channel master-level energy for the benefit of others. Because the master energy and its attunement address the soul level of healing, practitioner and client are supported to their highest potential. It's a path of discovery, healing and empowerment unique to each person

**How Reiki Works**
Reiki isn't a religion and requires no set belief system for it to work. It doesn't require meditations, incantations, rituals or ceremonies. You don't have to play music, burn candles or incense, or do anything special. All you do is intend to channel Reiki. Then place your hands on yourself, another person, a pet, a plant, your food, and the air around you in a room where you feel the energy is stagnant, dense or constricted. Or you direct it to a distant person, place or past or future event. The energy will follow the intention.

For a concrete example of how Reiki works, imagine a sphere of light in the sky above you. This light is the intelligent source of Reiki energy. That Reiki has its own intelligence is fundamental to any Reiki practice. You communicate to that light in whatever way is harmonious to you, intending to channel its energy at that moment to benefit another. The ball of Reiki energy sends out a beam of light/energy that travels from it to you. The light/energy enters through the top of your head, passes through your heart and arms and then radiates from your hands, penetrating whatever you place them on.

That's all. Nothing else is needed. The energy is fueled by your intention. It's believed that Reiki energy travels to wherever it will do most good, directed innately by the intelligence of the energy itself. The Reiki practitioner can place his or her hands on the client's head, but the energy may go to their arms, chest, back, or feet. The higher self of the recipient moves into direct relationship with the energy. The energy knows exactly where it's needed and goes there, regardless of where the practitioner's hands are placed. A Reiki practitioner is nothing more than a hollow reed, allowing the energy to pass through one's own body to another person.

Another way of looking at it is to imagine that Reiki is a natural healing life force that should be part of us all, but as modern life moves us away from nature, we are cut off from that energy. Through the attunement process, the Reiki practitioner gains access to this energy again. When the practitioner intends the energy to benefit someone else, the connection to this life force is once again awakened in the recipient. A vortex is created where the practitioner's touch on the client's body not only introduces Reiki into the client, but allows the Reiki energy to run on its own for the next day or so. The Reiki energy will balance the physical systems, flush toxins on all levels, help calm the mind and open the heart. It's important to remember though, the Reiki practitioner acts only as a conduit allowing the energy to pass through.

The Reiki energy practitioner doesn't amplify or direct personal energy but accesses universal power. Because this power has its own intelligence and works consistently to the receiver's highest benefit, Reiki is, or should be, a completely egoless modality. Anyone can study Reiki to a certain level, but practitioners personalizing Reiki's power, or seeking to bolster themselves through the identity of healer, miss the point. Such posturing affects the quality of the healing relationship but doesn't contaminate the Reiki that flows to, or activates within, the client. Over time, Reiki will expose and heal the practitioner's unconscious wounds, in the meanwhile working independent of who the healer is and what they do. But generally, the less doing and personalizing the better. Relaxing body and breath, releasing investment in outcome, being fully present and surrendering to the wisdom of each moment are key ingredients to maximizing the flow of Reiki energy.

**More About Reiki**

As this book focuses on expanding the context of Reiki and using other modalities to enhance it, we'll leave the details of performing Reiki to the many workbooks available on the market. But we'll highlight some important considerations for beginners.

Reiki energy can never harm and won't deplete your energy. You won't be placing your personal energy into the person you're working on and that person's energy can't back up into you. Reiki can be safely used as complementary treatment to whatever therapy your health practitioner recommends. As Reiki energy infuses the practitioner's body first, they receive healing energy while channeling energy to another. Reiki can be performed while the person is lying down, sitting up or in any position, and clients are always fully clothed. You can never do Reiki incorrectly as there's no wrong way to do it.

Most importantly, Reiki comes from the heart, not the head. Reiki reveals itself to you as you do and experience it. It is only illusion which separates us from universal life force energy and practicing Reiki helps us understand that we are Reiki. As we open to our true selves our intuition increases. Although some schools of Reiki prescribe hand positions not to be deviated from, *Shamanic Reiki* invites you to open your heart and let your intuition guide you. If you're working on a person's stomach and you feel the impulse to move to their feet then back to their stomach, do it. If you're drawn to resting one hand on their stomach and sliding the other one under them against their back, do it. The aspect of you in consonance with spirit (a word you should define according to your own belief system) addresses the needs of each moment and often nudges you to do something you hadn't planned on. The less strategic your approach, the better. Invite your intuition, listen to spirit's nudge. Later in this book, you'll read our view that shamanism is a natural extension of Reiki and learn techniques to enhance your energy sessions. Opening to intuition will be very important.

## About Shamanism

Shamanism is one of the oldest forms of spirituality that exists today. It predates any organized religion, having its roots buried thousands of years in our past. When anthropologists began studying it, they discovered that shamans in cultures separated by thousands of miles and without knowledge of each other developed healing and ceremonial approaches that were almost identical. Shamans call upon the essential forces of nature such as the winds, sacred plants, smoke, rocks, animals, fire and rivers for healing. They call in helping spirits, exorcise harmful intrusions and balance energies through the vibration of drums, bells, rattles, movement, chanting and other methods. The similarities among diverse cultures indicate that shamanism was evolved by those connected to something greater than them. If shamanism were not universal how could ancestral peoples from places as far apart as South America, North America, Europe, Asia and Africa develop such similar ceremonies and rituals? We'll explore in detail some of these techniques and practices.

During the past few decades, there's been a major interest and rebirth of the practice of shamanism in North America and Europe. No longer contained within native villages of indigenous peoples, shamanic healers can book months in advance as indigenous and Anglo shamans alike teach westerners how to apply ancient approaches to help present-day dilemmas. Workshops often overflow with participants. Because shamanism works and shamanic approaches enhance a person's ability to seek and find their own answers to life problems, the practice has endured. Growing interest in shamanic view has proliferated in hundreds of books on the topic on library and bookstore shelves.

We won't add much to what's already written on the subject of shamanism, but invite you to open to wisdom that's been safely practiced for thousands of years. Indigenous shamanism teaches that nature can balance and revitalize and shift consciousness; it opens us to invisible and intrinsic energies that most of us are unaware of. As we each descend from shamanic peoples, expanding consciousness, healing ourselves and living harmoniously with the earth is our birthright and responsibility. The power is within.

For those of you who are new to shamanism, a working understanding of it will add to your healing basket. A healing basket is that body of knowledge you already possess and use in your healing practice. Every time you integrate something new through concrete learning or personal experience, it enhances what you already know and you add that wisdom, insight or technique to your healing basket.

## What Is A Shaman?

Leading world authority on shamanism John Perkins describes a shaman as someone who travels to the spirit world or alternate realities to retrieve power, energy and wisdom that can be used for the betterment of this world. We see how easily this definition can be applied to Dr Mikao Usui who received the Reiki symbols in a spiritual state of consciousness after fasting and meditating for 21 days on a sacred mountain in Japan. Traditionally shamans were not only the healers of their communities, but powerful agents of change, mediators between the physical and spirit worlds, and those who were responsible for keeping balance between people and nature. Today, as shamanic practitioners proliferate and the awareness of our impact on a finite planet grows, shamans direct their energies personally and locally, but also to benefit national and global situations. Shamanism's earth-honoring message is one we need.

Shamans have expanded sensory perception and an ecstatic relationship to nature and "unseen" realities. Consciously participating with these natural forces marks the special aptitude of the shaman. With many forms of spirituality and organized religion, you'll find firm opinions of what you should or shouldn't do. But as with Reiki, the truths of shamanism are discovered through direct personal relationship. Teachings and techniques are often secondary to firsthand knowing as power derives from feeling, experience and a deep attunement with natural forces.

The word shaman originated with the Tungus peoples of Siberia and equivalent terms are used around the world. The Andean Quechua Birdpeople of Ecuador use Yachak. The title of shaman was typically bestowed by elders or community members after years of apprenticeship, although prophecies and signs can reveal young shamans still in their mother's wombs. An accident, lengthy illness, near death episode or even brief periods of insanity can also catalyze a call to shamanism. In the Shor mountain region of Siberia, shamanic illnesses are initiations that open the doors to spirit. None of us wish for suffering, but indigenous shamanic cultures understood the spiritual signposts of trauma.

Many North Americans and Europeans offer shamanic apprenticeship programs. They can span a week to a year or longer. It's helpful to understand that just as Tibetan Buddhism has evolved and been influenced by the cultures it's penetrated, shamanism also adapts to present-day needs. While we don't believe that a person can become a full-fledged shaman in one or even in several weeks, anyone can be a shamanic practitioner. Shamanism is innate and despite not living in cultures that recognize and support the journey of initiation, we all experience them. It's our choice to walk through when spirit opens the door.

**What Is Alternate Reality?**
Shamanism is founded on the non-hierarchical view that all life, not just human life, has consciousness. As with Reiki, the intelligence that infuses life empowers the shaman to transmute disease and harmonize imbalance. This includes the air we breathe and the winds that cleanse our planet; the waters we drink and that flow over the earth's body; the fire from the sun that warms us and the fire of stars, volcanoes, deep recesses of the earth; the earth herself and plants, animals, rocks, minerals and trees, as well as ancestral, human and other spirits.

Interfacing with reality as we know it is the world of spirit. This is not a world of ghosts, goblins or evil beings waiting to pounce on us like a lion on a gazelle when we aren't looking or are in a frail and weakened state. The spirit world interfaces ours and everything within it can be communicated and interacted with. And we mean everything. As our goal isn't to write exclusively about shamanism, you can learn more by reading *Shamanism as a Spiritual Practice in Daily Life* by Tom Cowan, written by a compassionate and knowledgeable western shaman. There are also other wonderful resources at the end of this book.

## How To Access Alternate Reality

There are many ways to access alternate reality and one is to take a shamanic journey. By relaxing, closing your eyes and listening to a rhythmic beat, a light trance-state is induced. This is similar to the hypnogogic state in which images appear in your mind's eye just before falling asleep, only in trance you aren't sleeping. The Australian Aboriginal peoples called this the tasmic state referring to the dreamtime, the mutable world where our everyday, waking reality is shaped. Shamans believe the dream is everything; that everything in our world originates from a spiritual plane of energy that can be engaged with for healing and change. Once you close your eyes, simply open your mind and allow yourself to daydream – a practice every child is intimately familiar with. Just as we need to set our intent before channeling Reiki energy, we now set our intention to go on a shamanic journey, a conscious daydream fueled by our imagination. Our active, linear minds need to hear that we won't get lost and will stay aware of our body and surroundings. But for a few moments, we'll suspend belief in a solid reality to engage the interfacing reality called the spirit world.

Some shamans are explicit about how to enter the spirit world and what to do when you get there. Others continuously move in and out of trance as they work, guided as they go. We feel that there are few rules in shamanism so whatever way works for you that is the way you should do it.

A simple way to begin a shamanic journey is to imagine yourself at the base of your favorite tree. Remember that each of us is oriented differently, and if you don't see anything, that's okay. You may just know it's there, feel it, or intuit it being there. Imagine in whatever way that works for you that there's an opening into the ground where the trunk meets the earth and feel yourself entering into that opening, descending into the ground.

As the intellectual side of you may not easily accept the spirit world as valid and real, allow your thoughts, judgments and analyses to be suspended until you return. Is this real? Is this my imagination? Hundreds of first-time journeyers ask these questions and the answer is that it really doesn't matter. What's important is your experience and what's valid and true for you.

A city dweller may choose to go down into the earth via an elevator, an escalator, the entrance to the subway, or a drain in your home or on the street. Or, it can be a real hole at the roots of a tree as per above, a hole made by an animal, a waterfall, a space between two rocks. To enter that space, use the power of your imagination. Feel yourself shrinking until the space between two rocks becomes as large as a cave. Go into the cave and find a pathway down into the earth. Or jump into the waterfall, hitting the water and going deeper, into the earth. How you arrive isn't important. Because the spirit world is mutable and fueled by the power of your imagination, anything is possible. Eventually you'll come out somewhere and when you do, you'll be in alternate reality.

You'll have a new world to explore. Look at or sense what's around you. Try to determine where you are. You may find yourself in a forest, on a mountain or near a rushing stream. Everyone's journey is different, yet each will find they're exactly where they need to be. Everything that appears to you in the spirit world is intelligent, sentient and can be communicated and interacted with.

First journeys are often taken to connect with an animal guide, and to find one all you have to do is to intend for it to happen. Call out in the journey-space and ask a guide to appear. If one doesn't arrive, ask a tree, rock, flower or the wind to help you. Trust that a guide will appear.

As with all relationships your connection to your animal guide will deepen through time and commitment. In the beginning you may ask your guide simple questions such as, "Why are you here for me? What lessons do you have to teach? What's needed in my life right now?" Don't expect the answers to come in a foreign voice. Spirit usually answers in your own voice or through metaphor, symbols, archetypal or mythological symbols. Sometimes we don't hear anything or see images at all, but sense or intuit the answers, or experience our guides on levels beyond visual, verbal or mental communication.

**Wrapping It Up**

Now that you have a taste of the shamanic, if this is the first time you're reading about it, have patience if you're confused or disbelieving. Even with this little information, you'll be able to give your clients a deeper and more empowered sense of healing. Inviting people to journey invites them to participate in their own healing, a powerful healing agent.

Just as Reiki flows more freely when ego is relaxed, the same is true for shamanism. Reiki practitioners don't do anything but channel or open access to energy. It's the Reiki energy that does the work and indigenous shamans will tell you they simply channel or open access to spiritual energies to benefit others. The ability to heal comes from the elements and helping spirits. It's not the shaman, but their spiritual connection that's powerful. Shamanic practitioners are intermediaries, accessing the spirit world on behalf of others, themselves, future generations and the earth. We ask spirit to guide us and channel through us so we can accomplish the greatest good.

As a healer, whether Reiki, shamanic, energetic or other modality, we accept our unique relationship to the greater energies of the universe. We'll call it spirit but use any name you wish. When opening to spirit, we trust our intuition even when we're intuiting something contradictory to what others, such as our families, teachers, friends, culture, may be telling us. As we open our hearts, our intuition grows and takes us where it will. The spirit world infuses the shaman with the power, wisdom and energy to effect change in this world. We may have important physical teachers in this reality, but our most important relationship is to spirit, and the guidance we're offered.

Although it can be hard for practitioners to trust themselves, trust grows through experience. Through growing trust in spirit, we gain confidence to do the healing work we're called to do and to live the life we're meant to live.

# CHAPTER TWO

# REMOVING AND TRANSFORMING ENERGETIC INTRUSIONS

Many handbooks explain the fundamentals of shamanism and Reiki, what to do and how to perform each. This book isn't like those. Instead of telling you what to do we'll share what works in our own practices. We encourage you to read, contemplate and assimilate what we share, paying attention to what draws you and discerning for yourself what resonates and what doesn't. We all have unique philosophical frameworks and individual ways of approaching healing. If there's something you can add to your healing basket, add it. If it doesn't fit for you, then don't use it or adapt it in more inspiring ways. Altering a technique because it feels more right to you honors your intuition. What inspires these changes is the nudge from spirit we talked about in the last chapter. Pay attention to it.

In any healing session, regardless of the modality, there are three physical components: the client, the practitioner and the environment. Though in Reiki and shamanism, spirit is the prime mover, we believe the most effective healings empower the client. When the three basic components of a healing session are harmonious, acting as one, miracles can happen. Throughout this text, we'll discuss how each of these can be enhanced to create an experience that allows for just that.

Practitioners prepare for and do sessions in a myriad of ways. It's important to stress that rather than right, wrong or better ways, there are mainly different ways. Below you'll find some distinctive ideas and preparations for Shamanic Reiki sessions gleaned through many years of practice and experience.

**Before the Shamanic Reiki Session**
Modern Quechua Andeans, descendants of ancient Inca peoples, believe

a shaman's spirit can travel unobstructed through time and space. Many North Americans traveling to study with indigenous shamans report that they meet and are guided by these shamans in dreams before their physical meetings. In the same way that a shaman's spirit prepares and connects with those coming to see them, a person scheduling a Shamanic Reiki session sets their intentions, activating subtle, and sometimes not so subtle, healing forces within the spiritual reality. This can cause shifts in ordinary reality which may be experienced by the client from the time of their first phone conversation with us to when the session occurs. As these precursory energies begin circulating days, weeks or even months before the actual meeting, synchronicities and cleansings can manifest in the client's daily life. From the first contact when the healing begins, we make sure people are aware of this important time. Until we meet it's a good time to reflect on special dreams (keeping a pad and pen by their bed can be helpful) or new insights that arise about why they scheduled the appointment. We ask that they pay attention to unexpected events and honor whatever emotions bubble up. Strange and magical things can occur and people should take notice, for all are spirit's nudging. Nothing is coincidence. Everything happens for a reason, even if we're unaware of what the reason is. Later we'll invite clients to share whatever draws them about their experience during this time.

Eating healthily and drinking a lot of clean pure water detoxifies physical impurities, maximizing the healing benefits for the body. The client may also wish to keep a written journal during this phase.

When people are en-route to our healing space for their appointment they enter a more pronounced period, what we'll call a portal of opportunity. Whether walking, driving, flying or just riding a subway, the more consciously engaged clients are as they travel to us, the better. They should open their heart to what they really seek in life and what they hope to gain from the session. Given the proper space to open, this portal connects them to higher guidance, helps bring to the surface what needs healing and reaffirms their connection to the universe. The opportunity can be missed through distraction so we instruct people to stay grounded, but aware and open, when traveling to us. When driving they can turn off the radio, relax, appreciate the scenery and notice what they see and feel. If flying, walking or taking a bus, they're encouraged to feel, to stay centered despite what's happening around them, and open to the unexpected. Spirit often catches our attention through unexpected events, yet it's up to us to recognize the event as a message.

## Doing Shamanic Reiki

Now that we're ready to concentrate on specific Shamanic Reiki approaches, note that you'll find a section called "Concept" before each practice. Here we explain the shamanic root of each technique explored and introduce practices you might want to add to your healing basket. There are just as many views, ideas and interpretations about shamanic teachings as there are traditional branches of shamanism. Not all shamanic practitioners will agree with what we present but that's inconsequential. If you attended a seminar by the world's most influential spiritual leaders you wouldn't necessarily leave knowing which religion was best. But you may have a deeper appreciation for diverse beliefs, understanding that different doesn't mean wrong. The same is true for shamanic beliefs and techniques. They vary widely in the global shamanic community, yet when arising from the right intention they're all valid.

## Concept

Shamans and energy practitioners believe that every physical ailment has a corresponding imbalance in the spiritual world. The ailments first appear in the energetic realms. These imbalances restrict our life force, impact everything we do and if not addressed can eventually manifest as symptoms or dis-ease in our bodies. One problem that first appears energetically, affecting healthy engagement with life and eventually manifesting in our bodies, is called an intrusion. Typically, shamanic practitioners view intrusions as energies directed to us by malevolent, alien or unconscious external forces. This could be as objects imbedded in us from past life wounds or as disassociated emotions, thoughts and feelings congesting as tangible shapes and forms in spiritual reality. These are sometimes called entities when they attain their own consciousness. When shamans perform healing ceremonies, they often ask their guides to intercede on behalf of their client to heal problems in these spiritual or energetic realms. Once the energetic balance has been restored, healing can occur in this reality. Physical symptoms may disappear and life can be experienced more fully.

**Preparing to Exorcize Intrusions**

We use healing stones or crystals for this but healing stones don't have to come from sacred sites in the Andes, Amazon, Tibet or equally exotic places. We can find them in our own back yards or in parks in the center of a city. Just go for a walk in a park or the woods, or any place in nature. Quechua shamans call these sacred items huacas (wa-kas) and they help us in our healing work. You don't look for huacas in a traditional sense of trying to find something, as they prefer to come to you in their own way. If your intention is to use the huacas to benefit others through your healing work, just open to your intuition and they'll find you.

When inviting huacas to come to you, open your heart and intend to find stones to help in your healing practice. Then walk the land keeping a soft gaze, allowing your feet to go where your heart calls, not necessarily where the path is. Open your senses. Feel and have gratitude for the life all around you as your feet touch the earth, the sun and breezes touch your skin, the sounds of nature (birds, insects or rustling leaves) touch your ears, and the smells of nature's scents touch your nostrils. Let your eyes skim the surface of the land as you walk, and without consciously realizing it, your gaze will eventually settle on a stone. Sense if this is your healing huaca. If not, continue the process. If it is, pick it up and express gratitude to the earth by leaving a small piece of bread or some flower petals or a bit of loose tobacco in its place. Wash your stone and then cleanse its energy by setting it in the sun on a windowsill or soaking it in a bowl of sea salt water 24 hours. When cleansed, place the stone on your altar or in a special place designated for your huacas.

If you prefer using crystals, black tourmaline is excellent for removing intrusions. It's a wonderful absorber of heavy energy because it never holds onto it. Instead, the tourmaline continuously transmutes heavy energy and returns it to the universal source so its flow is beneficial. This technically means it doesn't have to be cleared or cleansed, but we cleanse the tourmaline anyway. If you can't get a piece of black tourmaline, any quartz or other crystal you're connected to will work just as well. You should cleanse and clear the energy from those crystals after each use.

We also prepare a glass bowl filled with fresh, pure water that's infused with sea salt for our work in exorcising intrusions. We place this on the floor or on a small table next to our Reiki table so we can cleanse the stone or crystal we're using when we're finished.

## Locating the Intrusion

After channeling Reiki energy long enough so the client is completely relaxed, we invite them to do a simple visualization. We ask our clients to imagine rising up from the table towards the ceiling. Then, we ask that they turn around and look at themselves from above, pretending the body they look down upon is made of clear quartz crystal or glass. When looking at their clear crystal or glass body, we ask if they notice anything that doesn't belong or that no longer serves them. Usually this manifests as a non-physical object or colored shape, often, yet not exclusively, lodged in or around major organs. Each time we've facilitated this exercise clients see or sense a shape somewhere in their imagined crystal body. Just as the Reiki practitioner's intention activates Reiki energy, shamanic practitioners empower shamanic techniques through intention. When we suggest clients look for the spiritual aspect or cause of a pain in their shoulder, for example, they'll see it. If they don't see it right away, we suggest they imagine or make it up to relax the censoring aspect of their mind. The manifestation they sense or see can appear anywhere in the body despite symptoms or problems presenting elsewhere.

## Neutralizing the Intrusion

Once the client clearly sees or senses the shape or object, we ask them to describe it. If their description is vague, we'll ask what color it is, what it feels like, if the surface is rough or smooth, the edges round or jagged, and if it had a temperature would it be cold or hot? The client must gain a clear view or feeling sense of the form. Now we suggest they can change the object by intending so. Our wish is for them to change the characteristics of the spiritual intrusion into more neutral aspects. If the color is dark, we ask that they lighten it. If it's bright, we invite them to mute it. If the edges are sharp, smooth them. If the client says the object is cold we ask if they'd like to warm it, if hot, to cool it. If it's very large, we suggest they reduce the size. The point of this is to let the person know that through their intention they can affect the intrusion. This is empowering. So often it seems we can do nothing about what impacts us – the train is late, the traffic accident makes us sit in the car an extra half hour, or the rain postpones an outdoor event. In this exercise, the client not only visualizes the intrusion, but through the power of their will they can alter it. They're not merely recipients or spectators, but active participants.

The person we're working with lets us know when they've accomplished the task. Even those who've never heard of shamanism are able to locate and alter shapes they sensed within themselves. During this entire process we've continued channeling Reiki energy.

**Removing the Intrusion**

We first place our hand over the area of the intrusion. If it's in an area that's inappropriate to touch we ask the client to place their own hand there while we place ours slightly above it, continuing to channel Reiki energy. We then suggest that they intend for the intrusion to follow the hand as we or they slowly slide it away and toward the right side of their body. If they're moving their own hand, we take over at a place that's appropriate to continue, allowing them to relax again into the journey or visualization as we continue.

Our goal is to move the object towards the right shoulder, down their right arm, and into their hand. It's important to move the intrusion away from the client's heart, so we always move it to the client's right side before moving it up to their shoulder. Sliding our hand back and forth several times before guiding it toward their shoulder loosens the intrusion so we're able to move it. We continually check in with the clients as we proceed, asking them where the intrusion is and if it's moving in concert with our hand. In most instances, the shape or object will move.

Once the intrusion is located in the client's right shoulder, we guide it towards their hand. When ready to do this, we'll place a healing rock or crystal into the client's hand, telling them that they should visualize the intrusion dissolving into it. As soon as the rock or crystal absorbs the intrusion we ask our client to open their hand and drop the stone. We immediately collect then drop it into the bowl of sea salt water near the Reiki table. This completely cleanses the rock. Be aware that energy is not intrinsically good or bad, so as the sea salt water cleanses the rock, any harmful energy from the intrusion is released and re-cycled back into the universal energy field.

We then ask our client to imagine a beam of light emerging from deep within the earth's molten core, rising from her center through many layers, finally coming up through the earth's surface to infuse the person's body with light. We ask them to feel the warmth of this light as it fills them inside and out. We explain that nature doesn't like a vacuum, and invite them to intend and visualize this light completely filling the space within them that the intrusion occupied. While doing this we hold our hands over the area where the intrusion was and channel Reiki. When the client says the area is filled with light, we ask them to see the light beam retreat back into the earth. Then we continue the Reiki session. After the session is complete, we'll invite the client to share what they felt during this process.

It's not necessary for us or the client to understand the nature of the intrusion, though gaining that knowledge can be insightful. What's most important is that the energetic intrusion has been removed and the client's life force can now flow freely encouraging healthy, balanced patterns in this reality. Having the information can be a bonus, but not having it isn't an obstacle to healing.

## When Intrusions Don't Move

What happens if the intrusion doesn't move? We take our healing stone and place it over the intrusion. Then we tell the client that when we press in slightly, we wish him/her to visualize the stone acting like a magnet, pulling the intrusion out of them. We explain that as the stone (or crystal) is from mother earth, its power to heal comes from her. The intrusion, no matter how deeply embedded, won't be able to withstand the magnetic effect the rock or crystal has on it. Usually after gently pressing the stone a few times, the client tells us the intrusion is in the stone. We'll then place the stone into the bowl of sea salt water.

Although this is a simpler way of removing intrusions, we prefer having people remove it themselves. In doing so, they become an active force in their own healing. One of the reasons Shamanic Reiki is so powerful is that it empowers people in ways Reiki alone cannot do.

**For the Advanced Shamanic Reiki Practitioner**
As noted, clients are usually able to remove intrusions themselves. But if the intrusion is still not completely gone, we use a technique rarely employed through our years of practicing Shamanic Reiki.

When unhealthy energy forms resist moving out of the body on their own, Shuar Amazonian shamans will suck them out. To prevent ingesting the harmful energy into themselves in the process, they cough up protective invisible darts that were blown into them by their shamanic elders. The darts reach maturity through years of apprenticeship training and when ready, the shamans are able to regurgitate them up from their hearts and into their throats as healing tools. When this happens, no energies can harm them as they suck to draw intrusions from their patient then simply spit them out. Often, small physical objects fly out of their mouths onto the ground as they do this because the intrusions are energy forms which can also manifest physically. The objects are neutralized in the process and can cause no further harm because the energy is absorbed and transmuted by the darts.

But we have no darts within our hearts and neither do you. So, we employ a similar process but utilize our stone or crystal to absorb and transmute the energy of the intrusion instead of invisible darts like the Shuar. If you feel this is harmonious with you and worth putting into your healing basket, you may wish to try it.

We place the stone over the intrusion and let the client know we'll be sucking the remainder of it out and into the stone or crystal. We instruct them to breathe out forcefully when they hear us doing this to help move the energy and to imagine the intrusion being sucked up into the stone. After placing the stone on the intrusion we position our mouth completely on the stone. (We have several, and if the stone we were using as a magnet is too small, we replace it with a larger one. When searching for your own huaca, it's a good idea to intend to find several.) We connect with our guides, asking them to be aware of what we're doing and to reinforce the stone or crystal so the intrusion is sure to remain in it. As the stone or crystal is an extension of the earth, when we use them we're invoking the power of mother earth herself. She absorbs all the energy so we know none of it penetrates us beyond the barrier of the stone. We may have to suck once or twice before the intrusion is in the stone. When it is, we immediately drop the stone or crystal into the sea-salt water bowl. Then we face a window and expel a forceful breath, releasing out into the atmosphere residual but harmless energies.

## Understanding Intrusions

When clients are shamanic practitioners or practiced in shamanic journeying, the journeying process can help them understand the nature of their intrusions. However, through guided meditations we can take people to the same place a shamanic practitioner journeys to and the results are just as valid.

In the *Neutralizing the Intrusions* section, after the person you're working with has located the intrusion and neutralized its properties we ask if they wish to know more about it. When and why did it begin? How did it form and how can they avoid something similar manifesting again? If they're interested, we invite them on a brief shamanic journey to their guides and then into the intrusion itself. As everything has a consciousness that can be communicated with, once within the intrusion they'll dialogue with the non-physical object to learn what they can. Armed with awareness, clients can choose to think, respond and act in ways that prevent intrusions from returning. Gaining understanding is empowering and we encourage people to take such responsibility for their well-being.

Before a client leaves the shamanic journey space (or we bring their guided meditation to a close), they thank the intrusion for its insights and explain that since it no longer serves their higher good, they're inviting it to rejoin universal energy. Releasing from love and thankfulness is more powerful than releasing from anger.

If the client isn't experienced in journeying or doesn't wish to journey or meditate to the intrusion, we sometimes ask their permission to journey for them to retrieve information from the intrusion. Based on your level of shamanic experience, you may wish to do the same. In such cases we'll do a short journey while we continue to channel Reiki, and when the journey's done, we'll move the intrusion out of the body with the client's help. In either scenario, we discuss the journey and insights received only after the session is complete. But again, although this information can be helpful, it's not necessary to affect healing in this reality.

**Intrusions, a Non-Dual View**
In review, intrusions are tangible shapes and forms that exist in the spiritual reality, causing imbalances that impact us in this reality. These can eventually manifest as health and other problems. Shamans usually regard intrusions as alien and negative forces needing removal for the client's well-being. But as we gain a deeper feeling for the oneness of life (our connection to spirit, the universe, earth, or however you define or experience this oneness) we may see intrusions from a different perspective and let go of seeing ourselves as victims.

Whatever their origin, intrusions exist on some level at our invitation. Like attracts like, so whatever's un-healed or within our shadow selves invites forms, energies and experiences of a similar vibration. These may find a safe harbor within us. Where intrusions live are typically those areas of our body where our breath is restricted, those parts devoid of touch and where physical symptoms begin. No matter where they came from, when they've implanted or taken shape within us, they're ours to reckon with. But intrusions can be key holders to denied aspects, suppressed emotions and repressed life force. As said in *Removing the Intrusion*, energy is not intrinsically good or bad but part of the greater oneness. Therefore, instead of getting rid of intrusive forms, it's equally effective to transmute them as a means of reconnecting with aspects of ourselves we're cut off from. When we do so, these new energies can strengthen instead of deplete us.

**Transmuting Energetic Intrusions**
To transmute intrusions, we channel Reiki energy until our client is completely relaxed, then follow the section entitled *Locating the Intrusion*. When an intrusion is located we'll ask the person to rest their awareness in this part of their body, simply noticing what they're feeling here. We'll invite them to place their hands in this location if that's comfortable for them, and also ask if it's okay to rest our hands on top of theirs while continuing to channel Reiki. We invite them to notice, feel, and be present to the sensations in this part of their body. This alone can be a healing experience.

After some time we'll ask our client to invite communication from this part of their body. If the intrusion is located in their stomach area we'll ask, "If your stomach could speak, what would it say?" If nothing comes we invite them to make it up or to free-associate. This cuts through the tendency to discount what comes to them and opens the emotional tone associated with this part of their body.

You may remember that in the section, *Neutralizing the Intrusion* we explain how the client, through visualization, could alter the nature of the intrusion before ultimately removing it. To transform the intrusion, we follow the same steps from that section. This helps the client understand that the form is mutable and they can impact it. But instead of removing the intrusion, we follow this formula.

In this process, after they've changed the nature of the intrusion to the most neutral characteristics they can manage, we invite clients to imagine sinking into their bodies, stopping at the intrusion. We remind them that they can control the intrusion. From their new vantage point within their body we encourage them to see, feel or sense their control. This will remove any fear they might have of the intrusion.

We'll then invite them to walk into the intrusion. We tell them that what they first experience could be unsettling (being on a beach in a storm, over-looking a bleak landscape torched by fire and devoid of life, in a dark abandoned cave, etc.) because the energy associated with the intrusion is unconscious and lies in shadow. We assure them that they are fully protected as they enter and can stop the experience at any time, as they have control. They can also take a spirit, animal guide or any kind of healing tool in with them.

Once within the intrusion, the client is encouraged to describe what they see, feel and experience as they explore this space. Then, through intention, to change what they sense from within just as they changed what they sensed from without. They can alter any aspect they want and use healing tools or guides to assist them. For example, they can change the storm to a sunny day, watch flowers, bushes and new life spring up from the blackened ground, or they can intend a stairway to appear in the cave that leads them to a lighted opening. We remind them as they tell us what's occurring within their imagination that this is their dream and they can shape it as they wish. Once it's changed and they're happy and complete with the transformed energy, we invite them to stay there for a few minutes, feeling energy and being renewed by it while we continue channeling Reiki. It's then up to the client to decide if they wish to remove the new positive form or consciously give it permission to stay. Staying is a good thing because in reclaiming this part of themselves, they can return to the transmuted form on their own, whenever they wish, to energize and renew.

In our own practices we usually don't know which technique (removing or transmuting) we'll use before beginning a session. But in speaking with our client and observing them, or while we're channeling Reiki energy, we may sense there's an intrusion. Our attention is often magnetically drawn to these areas or we may feel a tug in our own body that mirrors where an intrusion is located in our client's body. We experience this as the form calling us to help release or transform it. Just as all of this happens, we also sense which approach to use. Experience has taught us to trust our feelings, intuition, and that both approaches work. Most important is to trust spirit to guide and work through us.

# CHAPTER THREE

# REMOVING DELETERIOUS ENERGETIC CORDS

As our practices evolved through years of integrating shamanic approaches with Reiki, the nature of our sessions changed, as did our relationships with clients. The work grew intimate and intense, making us aware of multi-layered emotional issues compelling people to seek more than Reiki. People were challenged in trying to free themselves of deeply ingrained unconscious patterns, often referred to as personal baggage. As they removed or transformed one layer of personal baggage, i.e. thoughts, emotions and habit patterns that limited their expression, they'd soon find deeper and different layers of baggage lurking just beneath the surface.

Unraveling these layers of personality can feel never-ending because habituated patterns are deeply identified with sense of self. It takes a modicum of self-reflection to acknowledge our limitations enough to say "This is just who I am." Yet if we go deeper into the nature of our issues we usually find the truer statement is, "This is who I choose to be." Discovering that who we are is a choice and knowing that we have power over our thoughts, feelings and responses helps us take personal responsibility. This frees us to consciously shape our lives and create a world reflecting deeper dreams and values.

To illustrate this we'll share an example. An introverted person may have adopted shyness as a protective mechanism when young. Although children usually can't control their environments they can control their internal state. It can be an intelligent strategy to adopt behavior patterns that make them invisible in the face of unpleasant circumstances. Or maybe being quiet was the reinforced or accepted mode of behavior for children, communicated to them by their parents, teachers and community. In either scenario, externally imposed behavior patterns mask the essence of the child who may or may not have an intrinsically quiet nature.

By the time we reach adulthood the original circumstances that molded our personalities are gone, but how we behave, respond and create our environments reflects what mechanisms are still in place. It's easy to give in by saying that we're shy or some other trait and that we can't do anything about it. It's harder to venture more deeply into why we are who we are, seeing which behaviors and views are shaped by the unconscious and conscious motives of others. Harder, yet more important, is unraveling societal layers, which unless exposed and circumvented, disassociate us, destroy nature and threaten our future generations.

"I like my quiet nature, but shyness prevents me from expressing what's important to me. I'm shy, but I'm going to shift this trait because being shy no longer suits me." With this admission, we accept who we are and in taking responsibility for ourselves, we can begin to shift into who we want to be. The first step of any new endeavor is usually the most difficult, and this is no exception. But when we surrender and recognize that the path we walk is spiritual, all things become possible. We then look at ourselves from new perspectives that illuminate our intentions to change who we are, and even change the world, as within our grasp.

**The Practitioner's Role**
As we affirm our commitment to being a healer and helper, we see we're inherently responsible for addressing whatever comes up for clients in the course of our work with them. This may seem obvious, but we've heard of cases where it isn't.

An acquaintance went to see a shamanic practitioner for help. After the session the person felt ungrounded and disoriented. After two days of feeling out of sorts, the person left a phone message for the shamanic practitioner asking for help. The practitioner didn't call back. Only after several more attempts and several more days of feeling disconnected, did the two speak. The practitioner's response to the client's concern was that sometimes this happens. No helpful suggestions were offered except that it would be good to come in for another session but this couldn't happen for another week due to the practitioner's busy schedule. This meant the person was uncomfortable, disconnected and disoriented for another seven days. There's something wrong with this approach. If we open a door with a client, we must see them safely through that door. We don't have to be perfectly healed ourselves to do healing work with others, but practitioners must be aware of their own blind spots. For clients to feel secure they should know how to reach us after or in between sessions if needed, and we must respond to their calls in a timely fashion.

As Shamanic Reiki practitioners, we actively engage the deeper causes of imbalance as well as those that perpetuate unhappiness for our clients. In doing so, we've seen that people need more than just Reiki treatments to become who they really want to be and to interact with the world meaningfully. Our goal to empower people shifted our work from its early beginnings of "lie on the table and receive Reiki energy" to one incorporating many approaches, addressing personal ills inseparably from societal and global imbalances. This increased our responsibility as healers, highlighting the importance of holding unconditional space for whatever may come up in a session. Becoming aware of how our own projections and issues impacted our work with others helped us do this more effectively. As you gain experience as a Shamanic Reiki practitioner, you'll discover that self-awareness is the key to holding a genuine healing space for others.

We also began spending more time with people, scheduling longer appointments with them. We found two to four hours optimal. This ran contrary to models set by some of the most recognized healers in North America, most notably, psychotherapists, psychiatrists and psychologists. Fifty minutes was, and still is the classic therapeutic hour dutifully honored by even many alternative and Reiki healing practitioners. There are practical considerations for this time frame such as insurance dictates, finances, client load and prescribed ideas about professional boundaries. The hour block has its own wisdom but we should be clear this is modern phenomenon and no magical formula. Certainly this isn't what helping people looks like across historical and geographical boundaries.

In the high Andes, Quechua people will arrive at the humble home of their local shaman with chickens, eggs and home-brewed sugar-cane alcohol as offerings, not for the person who performs the healing for them, but for the shaman to accept from the client on behalf of the sacred volcanoes, spirits and natural energies that will act through the shaman for the person's benefit. The healing space is rustic. Neighborhood children may be playing in a corner of the room, dogs and chickens may occasionally stray in and out, and the shaman's wife and daughter in-law may be preparing food over a low, traditional fire in the next room. The *Yachak* (Quechua word for shaman) wears a watch yet doesn't take note of the time, nor does he know his clients are coming until they show up at his door. He greets them warmly as if they're family members and asks them to explain what's troubling them and why they've come to him. The Yachak spends the next hour or two, or as long as it takes to offer a healing ceremony and help those who find their way to him.

We aren't indigenous Yachaks and don't live high in the Andes, but appreciating how shamanic healers have helped people for centuries can support us when we're nudged by spirit to do something different, like spending the time we feel is needed to help our clients.

A colleague of ours, an acupuncturist, was frustrated with her practice until she followed our example by lengthening her sessions. The option had never dawned on her, so unconsciously invested was she in accepted time parameters around visits. As soon as this woman began taking more time with her patients her work with them grew more relaxed and thorough, and her intuition increased. The acupuncturist was happier to be more in tune with the people she worked with, which also produced good results for them.

If this is something that resonates with you, taking more time for your Shamanic Reiki sessions and using that time well, you may find you engage people more thoroughly in the session, and empower them to continue the work after leaving your healing space. Throughout this book, we offer concrete tools to this effect that you can add to your healing basket.

**Being a Spiritual Counselor**

Being a Shamanic Reiki practitioner doesn't require us to be psychotherapists. People come to Reiki and shamanism from diverse walks of life, often practicing energy work in addition to trades and professions that have nothing to do with healing. This is also true of modern Quechua shamans who play ordinary roles in their community, donning the identity of healer only when needed. Many are farmers and merchants, called in from the fields or to the back of the shop when people arrive for their services. This makes it hard to place these shamans on pedestals, keeping them balanced and simpatico with their community.

But as Shamanic Reiki practitioners we do need to recognize our helping role can cross over into what we might call spiritual counseling. Though thinking of ourselves as being spiritual counselors might be intimidating, we can trust our ability to make the transition. No matter our background, we all come to Reiki and/or shamanism from a wealth of life experience. By trusting our experience, listening to spirit's nudge, and in attending to our client's words, body language and energy, we can offer support and encourage healthy approaches to any dilemma. Insights may arise or we may sense something in our heart, intuition or from helping energies. We trust the source of these insights is spirit. Insights that may arise and resonate for our client could be perspectives that help them break through personal barriers to change problematic behavior, or that help them relax enough to accept things for what they are. Shamanic Reiki practitioners don't tell clients what to do and only mindfully disclose what they intuit. We invite people to share their journey with us and we support the changes they desire to make. Using practices discussed in this text, we help people become more aware and dissolve or change what gets in their way. It is they who do and direct the work; we simply facilitate their ability to do this. Suspending our own interpretations and conclusions is fundamental to holding the space for this to happen.

**Personal Energy Dynamics**

As noted in the first chapter, the practice of Reiki is channeling universal life force energy to benefit another person, plant, animal and so forth, and across time and space. There are other types of energy, personal energy that's different from Reiki, that each of us can radiate and draw on. Have you ever been in a good mood, entered a room filled with people and suddenly realized that you weren't feeling good anymore? Or has the opposite happened, have you entered a room feeling upset or angry but soon found yourself feeling better? And did both happen before you even said your first hello? One of the suppositions behind this is that people give off and take in energy, many times without being consciously aware of it. The happy person exudes happiness, releasing life-affirming energy, while the sad, angry or wounded person can radiate waves of discordant or heavy energy – or actually draw energy to them from another. If you're in the path of, and open to releasing energy, you may be affected by it. If you participate with, or are victim to an energy *taker*, you may become drained.

We each have the ability to release and draw energy – we all do it. This energy can be benign or not. The energy we release is often uncon-scious, that is, not borne from conscious intention. But regardless of how or why they're generated, energy exchanges between people are often not in either party's best interest. Experiencing the unconscious draw of energy and what are known as energy-draining cords is never healthy, yet offers important lessons regarding our own power as well as ways that we may undermine others. In this chapter we'll explore how to remove undesirable energy connections during a Shamanic Reiki session.

A client once came to a healing session fuming in anger. She indicated the source of her anger was her Qigong teacher who said something that made her explode. In speaking about this with the person, it became obvious that her reaction wasn't proportionate to what had happened. Fortunately, this soon became apparent to her as well. Where did all of this anger come from? When encouraged to explore this, the woman mentioned her verbally abusive mother. After continuing the conversation for a few moments we suggested, "Is it possible that your Qigong teacher triggered old wounds concerning your mother? Is it also possible that when you yelled at your Qigong teacher you were, in effect, yelling at your mother?" The client readily agreed, and in doing so, brought to light an unconscious layer waiting to being healed, the negative attachment between her and her mother.

## Concept

Dark, energetic cords exist and connect us deleteriously to people we knew in the past or know in the present. These cords may occur between parent and child, friends or lovers, bosses and employees, therapist or healer and client. Healthy, mutually beneficial, life-affirming relationships manifest connections that appear as luminous strands between people, but when relationships aren't serving the higher good, their bonds form into dark, knotted cords, draining energy and personal power. Dark cords form between those harboring unconscious expectations, projections, unhealed emotional wounds, and they can form quickly. As the energy of dark corded bonds adversely affect well-being, it's important to become aware of and disconnect them. Practitioners, as well, must take responsibility to work with their own unconscious expectations and projections. Similar to intrusions, cords don't happen without our participation, although some are more pervasive and controlling than others. But unconscious, menacing or otherwise, we can remove dark cords using shamanic techniques.

One specific example of this dynamic is a mother's connection to her child. If the mother has a healthy relationship with her young child, there will be a luminous and nurturing bond between them. But if the mother has unhealed wounds about being held back by her own parents as she grew into adulthood, the maturing child may trigger the mother's powerlessness. If this dynamic remains unconscious and unaddressed, the mother may try to manipulate the young person to prevent their autonomy. In this case, the mother's attachment burdens the child, now turning adult, manifesting as a dark, energetic cord between them. The mother may still want the best for her child, but defines this according to her own terms. The success of her unconscious attempt to undermine is dependent on the child's power over, or resilience to, what's happening between them. Cords come from, and attach to, resonant areas of powerlessness.

Another short and somewhat different example is in the workplace. A person denied a promotion might feel jealous of the person promoted. If the energy of that jealousy unconsciously resonates with feelings of guilt or unworthiness in the newly promoted person, it can negatively impact both parties.

**Preparing to Remove Energetic Cords**

There are several approaches to removing energetic cords, and as we present them, understand that none may be what you choose. Once you glean the gist of the process from our descriptions, you may be guided to remove cords your own way. Shamanic Reiki healing comes from the heart not the head, and this isn't a do as we do manual. We'll offer some powerful ways to remove unwanted energies to add to your healing basket, or you can evolve alternate ways to do the same thing.

Again, it's important that our client is totally relaxed, so we suggest waiting at least 15 minutes into the Reiki session. Reiki sessions in and of themselves will over time loosen and remove energetic cords, but the shamanic process is expedient and empowers the client through conscious participation. At the same time, there are specific benefits to using shamanic methods to remove intrusions and cords during a Reiki session. Channeling Reiki relaxes the client and practitioner and opens psychic channels, making shamanic realms accessible. Reiki raises the vibration of the energy fields of the environment, facilitator and recipient supporting the more dynamic shamanic approaches. Reiki carries inherent protection from taking on releasing energies and helps people ground and integrate the rapid changes that can occur in using shamanic practice.

When the person is totally relaxed and we feel ready to begin the shamanic approach, we begin the same way we did before. We ask the client to imagine lifting out of their body and turning around to face themselves once they near the ceiling. It's not necessary this time that they imagine their body is made out of crystal. The person is simply asked to concentrate on their body and look at or sense it very carefully. They are looking for, or feeling for, psychic/energetic cords that have imbedded in their body. Please note that sensitive people may see and sense cords without rising up and visualizing their bodies. Many people know and feel where life draining cords are attached, as well as during which interactions, and to whom, they've connected. They may even feel the psychic energies coming into their bodies. If we find that's the case, the visualization isn't needed.

### Removing Energetic Cords

It's important to remember the power of intention in Reiki and shamanic healing. We make sure the person is aware of this and ask them to state their intention to the universe. In this approach, simply stating "I wish to see the energetic cords attached to me," isn't enough. They must be specific. If the client and we determine that a particular individual placed the cords, the client must include the person's name in their statement of intent. "I wish to see the energetic cords that my mother attached to me." We tell the client that the cords are usually identified as dark, long bundles; the more pervasive ones will have roots penetrating into the body around glands, organs, or some other part. Cords will most often appear in weak areas of the body or the energetic system.

Once the person tells us they see or have a felt sense of a cord, we ask where on their body it's attached. If possible, we place our hands there and continue to channel Reiki energy. For Level Two practitioners or above, we then draw the power symbol over the area and gently tap the symbol into the client's body three times, silently repeating the symbol's name three times with each tap. We may be drawn to doing the same now, or later, with other Reiki symbols. The symbols can also be visualized at any time we're intuitively drawn, and by our intention the symbols can be projected into the client's body anywhere we're guided to do so.

Then we'll ask the client if they wish to remove the energetic cords. If they say yes, we'll hand them a helpful tool. This may be a stick, a feather, a butter knife or anything that helps the client see in their mind's eye, or have a strong sense of the cords being severed. Alternately, sometimes we use a crystal or our healing rock, asking that as the crystal or rock touches the cords, they imagine the cord responding like hair against a flame, immediately shriveling and disappearing back to where it came. We ask the client to clearly see or feel the cords disconnecting as they pass the tool or crystal over their body. When the area we're working on looks or feels clear and the client says there are no more cords, we'll continue giving Reiki to that area. Then we'll ask the client to do the same exercise we explained in Chapter Two, to see or feel the light rising from the center of the earth, entering and filling the area the cords used to occupy.

## Removing Both Ends of Cords

Removing energetic cords is an example of how Shamanic Reiki can empower clients in ways that Reiki alone can't. This next practice can transform those who are ready for it.

Before asking a person to remove cords we'll let them know they can actively reclaim their personal power by removing cords from both ends. If they agree to this, we'll ask the client to imagine grabbing a single cord of energy, then traveling out along that cord until they reach the person who sent it. When they see, sense or intuit the person, tell them that they are seeing or sensing the person's higher self, that aspect which perceives from the highest good and knows about the cords.

It's ideal when our clients dialogue with this higher aspect of the other person to understand the issues burdening each of them. In that dialogue, the client must trust that the issues, no matter how long standing, can be resolved. This way, when they ask that higher self to dissolve and detach all the energetic cords associated with these issues, the results are usually positive. We'll encourage people to release with love as they speak to the person's higher self, "Thank you for what you did, even if it wasn't in my best interest. I appreciate the lessons of this experience and have a greater understanding of my own role in it. But as these attachments prevent me from living life fully, I ask you to disconnect them." The attachments usually immediately fall away. This is the first step in freeing a person to experience renewed energy and power.

These aren't your words, they're ours. But understanding the meaning behind them is what's important. When you follow this procedure, whatever you invite your client to communicate to the higher self of the person at the other end of the energetic cord will be just the words that are needed.

After our client lets us know the person's higher self has cut the cord from the initiator's end, we'll ask that they bring their awareness back into the room so they can cut the cord on the other end, the cord they see, or sense, which is attached to their own body. To do this, we follow the steps in the last paragraph of the section entitled *Removing Energetic Cords*.

**Alternate Scenarios for Severing Cords**

In shamanic reality, time doesn't exist in the same way it does in ours. To the shaman, all times and spaces are accessible – past, present and future simultaneously occur. This same view empowers Reiki Level Two and Three practitioners to heal wounds from the distant past and to send Reiki to future events or to people and situations in need across the globe. That space doesn't obstruct energy and that time occurs simultaneously means the person who has attached cords to your client doesn't have to live close-by or even be alive. Even if the originator is dead, the cords may still exist, their pull and effect the same as if the person were alive. Our client will see or sense these energetic cords and the dialogue we'll invite them to have will be with the deceased person's higher self. These conversations can heal wounds and conflicts that people haven't been able to resolve in person, as those they involve are no longer alive. When the energetic attachments between them fall away, this frees our client to view the deceased person in a different light, opening the door to deeper healing.

And what if someone doesn't know where the cords originate? Intention is everything. In this case, the message sent to spirit is, "Show me attachments that no longer serve my higher good and that affect my life today." Once those cords are seen, the most empowering act is to ask the client to trace them back to see who's at the other end, as outlined above. They then dialogue with that higher self. But the person may not wish to trace the energy back, only remove it. In that case, we invite them to dislodge the cords and visualize or feel the earth's light entering and filling them, as described earlier. When done, we continue sending Reiki energy to the person and hold off further conversation until the session is over.

## Severing Cords, A Different View

As we've said many times, there are myriad ways these practices can be accomplished. Here's another way to help people remove cords without knowing their origin. Many times this is easier for people because knowing who they're attached to can make them harder to sever. This is often what's behind our client's reluctance to journey to the initiator of dark cords, and also why when we journey to them, we only engage the originator's higher self.

Imbalanced relationships, though dysfunctional, are seductive and can feel as comfortable as a second skin. As these ties evolve from, and are perpetuated through the disempowered aspects of people, the fear of what may change when they're removed can paralyze us. "If I remove the cords that propel me to please my father, will he remain in my life? If I sever the unhealthy ways my partner and I relate, what will be left? Will I still love and want to be with him/her?" Similar fears can prevent us from releasing unhealthy, unsustainable life-style patterns. Cords can keep us reactive and blind us to healthier ways. Our clients and we can also get psychically pulled in if the initiator, whether person, company, family or culture, senses things are changing. Because of these issues, and the fact that there are often many cords, we'll sometimes use a more expedient process to remove them.

The following technique is best used with clients you've established a strong relationship with.

Again, we'll channel Reiki energy a full 15 minutes until we are both thoroughly relaxed. We encourage them to feel, as we also feel, the palpable quality and power of Reiki energy as it completely fills and surrounds us, creating a brilliant, spiraling vortex of light in the room that continuously recycles and transmutes energy. We ask the person to clearly imagine this Reiki energy spiral and feel it with all their senses. Then we invite them to express to the universe that they wish to see or sense an energetic cord attached to them. They'll become aware of a cord and may also get an image of the initiator. In this scenario, however, knowing who it is isn't necessary and we encourage our client to stay present, not focusing their attention on the cords or the person, but on the Reiki energy, the light spiral, their intentions and actions.

We'll then ask the person to imagine reaching into their own body, physically going through the motion with their hands, to quickly and forcefully pull out the cord imbedded there. When the cord is removed, they'll immediately summon light from the earth to fill the void the cord has left in them, as we also place our hands there to channel Reiki energy. As soon as they feel the area is filled with light, and this can happen quickly, they ask the earth to now send light to the person at the other end of the cord. As they do this, we also ask for Reiki energy to go to the initiator.

In this approach, neither the client nor we focus much on the cord or the instigator of the cord, but simply intend and know that the earth and Reiki energy immerse the other person in healing light. This light encourages the other person's higher self to awaken and loosens the attachments so they come out more easily. We check in with our client, and when they feel the time is ripe, we'll ask them to reach out with their hands and with their imagination, to quickly and forcefully pull the cord out, now from the other end. As soon as this is accomplished, they'll throw the cord into the Reiki energy spiral in the room, which immediately lifts it up, out, and transmutes it without a trace remaining.

When this is accomplished, we invite the person to breathe deeply, feeling renewed and whole, as we smooth their energy field with a feather or our Reiki energy hands. Then we'll invite them to ask to see the next energetic cord that impacts them in ways that do not serve their highest good. Our clients and we repeat the steps in this section until all dark cords are removed.

Which method should you use? Only you and your intuition, in relationship to the needs and interactions of the person you're working with, can determine that. Most important is to trust that you'll be guided to do what's best for them.

# CHAPTER FOUR

# USING SHAMANIC REIKI TO SHIFT ENERGETIC BLOCKS

As you may have surmised by now, shamanism is a universe unto itself and as with Reiki, it's available to everyone. That's what makes both so fantastic. You don't have to be born into an indigenous tribe living along the Amazon River or the Mongolian border to access the wonders of shamanism in your healing practice. Everyone can create a working relationship with spirit and learn to trust that whatever happens in that relationship is exactly what's needed in our personal lives as well as in our healing practices.

So far, we've explained some shamanic concepts and shown you how those concepts can be used to expand work with clients in a Reiki setting. In this chapter, we'll introduce additional shamanic concepts which can be integrated with Reiki in whatever ways inspire you. If you're still feeling timid about learning shamanic approaches, now's the time to forget your inhibitions and jump in.

On a fundamental level, Shamanic Reiki means two things, being a Reiki practitioner who uses shamanic approaches, and being a shamanic practitioner who also utilizes Reiki. On a deeper level, Shamanic Reiki invites you to dissolve some of the boundaries you may perceive between Reiki and shamanism. Doing so opens us to the limitless ways we can work with the universal life force energy for the higher good, empowering our clients more fully than the laying on of hands alone can do.

It will help to understand a little more about indigenous perspectives, but before going further you should know this. If advertising strictly as a Reiki practitioner, it's important to speak with clients before sessions, asking them why they wish a healing and what they know of alternative healing. Healing is more than a brief introduction with a new client, a session, and then a departure. If, during that conversation, the person appears unfamiliar or uneasy with shamanism, or views it negatively, we'll use only the simplest approaches presented in this text. As the client-practitioner relationship deepens, we'll slowly suggest additional shamanic approaches. The reasons for this are obvious. To open to the universe for healing, clients must feel safe and comfortable under your care, and in the space you create for them. If you invited someone into your home knowing they had a passionate dislike for spinach, you wouldn't serve creamed spinach for dinner. The same etiquette holds true for healing sessions. But if the client is open to shamanism or if we're offering Shamanic Reiki and people know what to expect, we'll go with what moves us in the moment.

That last sentence exemplifies the key we wish to pass on – *we'll go with what moves us in the moment.* We spoke earlier about listening to spirit's nudge, about listening to and following your intuition. This is important because trusting yourself and trusting spirit, opens the door to Shamanic Reiki. Once you open that door your confidence will grow, allowing you to embrace a more dynamic path of healing. Intuition will guide you. Even if we tried, we couldn't detail every nuance of Shamanic Reiki healing anymore than we can give you insights that only personal experience can bring. Approaches are as diverse and unique as the practitioners, clients and circumstances that call them into action. Every moment unfolds freshly. We can share what we do and offer examples and explanations as springboards, but the rest must come from you and spirit.

We stated early on that there's no wrong way of doing Reiki and that the truths of shamanism are found through personal relationship. There's no wrong way of practicing Shamanic Reiki as long as your intent is pure and your approach supports the health and higher good of your client, not your own ego. The only additional quality needed is your openness and a personal relationship to spirit. Our partnership with spirit is forged through our own willingness and the integrity of our intent: the life and breath of spirit moves through us when we commit ourselves to benefiting others.

## The Universal Life Force is Universal

In Reiki, the universal life force is channeled through the hands of the Reiki practitioner for healing. As powerful as this practice is, it's also important to realize that indigenous peoples the world over have recognized and harnessed universal living energies for millennia. *Ushai* (oo-shy) is a Quechua word meaning the fifth element, the spirit that permeates all the elements, infusing us, and everything around us, with brilliant life force. By consciously connecting with ushai, we harmonize with the universal energy. Mongolian *hiimori* is windhorse energy. This energy is also known to those of the Siberian steppe and to the Tibetan peoples. Wind represents the vital force of life within and all around us. Horse symbolizes power, instinct, force, and the ability to navigate these vital forces in order to channel universal energy. Also from the Quechua, the word *Pachamama* roughly translated means mother earth, mother time and mother universe. Literally translated, Pachamama means the universal power of mother earth and mother time. We can't miss the striking similarities in these descriptions.

On the majestic slopes of the Himalayas a small group of Tibetan monks practice daily revitalization techniques meticulously passed down through centuries. The words Pachamama and Reiki aren't used, yet the practices evoke universal life force energies, directing them to flow through subtle channels within the monk's body. Simultaneously in a distant part of the world in the high Andes, a Peruvian woman reaches up to the heavens to collect and breathe in the vital universal energies. She brings those energies down through her body to energize and awaken the universal qualities within her. Not far away, in the Ecuadorian Andes, another shaman woman chants, calling on the powers of the volcanoes and Pachamama. She shapeshifts into and becomes one with these universal energies in order to channel that life force for her client. The woman then forcefully blows with the breath of spirit, *camaying* (Quechua word roughly translated to mean oneness) these energies into her client's heart, third eye and crown.

It is important to note that the act of blowing with the breath of spirit to transmit energy is not only observed in many indigenous shamanic groups as well as in eastern spiritual traditions, but it's also used in Reiki attunements. The Reiki master transmits, and infuses the student with, spiritual energy that's channeled through the vehicle of the master's breath. Shamanism and Reiki are related in many ways.

Pachamama. Windhorse. Reiki. Looking at the similarities in the examples above, one realizes these can't all be different energies. Ancient shamanic traditions utilizing life force energy have been handed down across divergent and widely separated cultures. Though they may have different approaches and perspectives in harmony with their own beliefs as well as different names and ways to access this energy, these differences don't impact the energy itself or the benefit to those evoking it.

Imagine a chef creating a large apple pie. Now imagine that people from all over the world who've never eaten apple pie are coming to taste it. They may name it differently, describe its taste in their own language, and even eat it differently according to the customs of their culture. But the source of their experience is the same apple pie. The same holds true for the universal life force. It remains the wakeful, primordial wind of universal energy within and all around us, an energy we can all access. Our approach may be different yet our experience can be as effective and positive as that of our ancestors. Knowing this intellectually is different from experiencing it viscerally, knowing it in our hearts and bodies. But as we bond with spirit and trust our intuition, new doors open. As they do, we glimpse abundant possibilities for channeling, amplifying and being guided by, the life-giving energy of the universe in Shamanic Reiki.

In Chapter Two we mentioned some objects that can help you and your clients remove intrusions and energy cords: crystals, stones, sticks and feathers. Do these carry power in and of themselves? Can items that come from nature – stones, sticks feathers, and others – transmit healing energy? Are some items intrinsically more powerful than others? Let's explore this.

## Concept

The power of our earth mother is magical as she comprises everything in our physical reality. Shamanic tools that come from the earth, plants, flowers, rocks or others, carry the same powers that infuse her. You can use these and other tools to help people just by intending for them to do so. Their connection to mother earth and the living energy that infuses her, allows this energy to be focused for greater well-being. In the simplest terms, all healing stems from the universal life force, Pachamama, Windhorse, Reiki, or whatever name we choose to call it. Shamanic Reiki practitioners are intermediaries between the client and this power source which enlivens everything on our planet and the universe. Tools from our earth mother are extensions of her, and transmit her energetic qualities as well as the energy that sources her.

How can you use this information in your healing practice? In Chapter Two we spoke about healing stones and offered one use for them, to aid the removal of spiritual intrusions identified by your client. Now we'll offer more ways Shamanic Reiki practitioners can use these and other tools. If you're wondering whether there's a big difference between you and indigenous shamans who also use these tools, there's very little. Granted shamans have apprenticed and trained for years in methods and intuitively know what to do and when to do it. But when placing a stone on a person and asking spirit to remove an energy block that experience and intuition helped them see, there's no real difference between the two of you in that moment. Neither of you are the force behind what healing that stone can facilitate. The element of earth the stone represents, and the universal forces that flow through her, are doing the healing.

The two main differences between you and that shaman are first, their unequivocal trust that mother earth and spiritual life force are working through the stone, doing whatever's needed for the higher good of the client; and second, their pervasive connection to spirit. You, who may just be opening to Shamanic Reiki, haven't yet developed that trust or relationship with spirit. The earth and universal energies do not hold back healing properties because of this. Your intention focuses the energy so the healing that's needed, happens. The same is true for Reiki practitioners as they all channel Reiki energy regardless of experience. But, not being seasoned shamans raised inseparably from spirit, we ask you to trust that bringing shamanism into a Reiki session grounds your work.

Once we open a Reiki session (and evoke the Reiki symbols for Level Two practitioners and above) everything we do happens under the umbrella of Reiki. This way, every shamanic element used is directed and guided by Reiki, the living universal intelligence. We can relax and trust the universe to work through us in dynamic ways. What arises is what each moment calls for.

A shaman's healing stones, feathers, drum, or sticks are no more powerful than our own or others' shamanic items. To demonstrate this, we'll share a story told by John Perkins, who's studied shamanism for almost 40 years in various parts of the world. Many years ago, a friend and acknowledged shaman from Ecuador visited John at his home in Florida. One day, John took the shaman to perform healings many miles away. Well into the ride, the shaman realized he'd forgotten his shamanic bag containing all his sacred stones and other healing tools. He didn't tell John to turn the car around so they could return to collect what he'd forgotten. Instead, they continued on and when they reached their desti-nation, the shaman went into the person's back yard, selected some stones and plants and leaves that he found, and used them in his healing. That healing was just as powerful as when the shaman used his own healing tools.

This example illustrates some important points. The shaman knew that as the earth and the energies that flow through her are the source of power of his huacas, the ones selected from a Florida backyard would be just as powerful. It's the shaman's intention and connection to spirit that's important, not where the objects he holds in his hands have come from.

And if the shaman were unable to retrieve any items at all, he could still do his healings. In such cases shamans access universal powers directly instead of focusing energy through huacas. Shamanic tools are focal points to concentrate energy, making it easier to accomplish what's needed. The same is true of the Reiki symbols which, through application and focus, are keys to empower specific directives for the universal life force energy. But it's important to remember that tools, symbols, stones and bells, are the channels and vehicles for the energy, not the energy itself. This shaman had a lifetime of experience enabling him to understand and trust this, and was raised in an environment that supported it. Given the time, and commitment to doing so, we can all forge such a trusting relationship with spirit.

## The Flow of Human Energy

Before progressing into how plants, stones and other items can be used in Shamanic Reiki, let's talk about the flow of human energy. In Chapter Two we discussed energetic intrusions and in Chapter Three we introduced the concept of energetic cords and how to remove them. Here, we'll add a little more to the concept of energy. Energy continuously enters, circulates through, and departs from the human body. This energy can include heat and light from the sun; energy created by other people, times and situations; energy from electronic machines, buildings, telephone wires and others; energy that filters to us from distant stars and that radiates through us from the core of the earth, as well as from the atmosphere and nature all around us. Our thoughts, emotions, actions, habits and how we respond to the events in our lives also impact how energy flows through us.

Popularized now is the energy circuit derived from the eastern yogic tradition known as the chakra system. The major chakra points are said to span from the base of our spine to the top of our head. Chakras are often described as spinning wheels of energy in our subtle body system; the major wheels metabolizing spiritual energies that filter through the endocrine glands to fuel the physical body. Unneeded energies also release through these spinning vortices, and other energies filter in and out of them, as well.

The ancient Chinese practice of acupuncture offers yet another way to view the flow of energy throughout the human body. Acupuncture is based on the premise that life force energy flows along energy meridians networked throughout the body, similar to the way blood flows through our veins. Yet one energy system is just as valid as the next and the most simplistic perspective is all that's needed for our purposes here. We take in or absorb energy then it moves through our bodies and out.

## Concept

Once within us, and for us to stay healthy, energy should flow smoothly throughout our body whether through chakras, meridians or whatever your conceptual model. Yet it often doesn't, and when this happens it's called an energy blockage. Root causes of blockages stem from physical, emotional, mental and spiritual imbalances or events. As an example, emotional shock or trauma, and rigid or negative attitudes create emotional energy blocks. Ingesting drugs, chemicals, or undergoing invasive medical procedures involving anesthesia can also lock energy in the body. Blocked energy indicates dis-harmony and dis-connection, manifesting on the spiritual plane first. If not corrected, the energetic imbalance may eventually express itself as a symptom or dis-ease.

Remember that everything originates on the spiritual plane. This means we can address energetic imbalances before they turn into physical problems. Once symptoms or dis-ease manifest, they can still be healed but it's generally more difficult. Ultimately, physical-level issues won't dissipate until the energetic flow is also balanced and restored. Working on the spiritual plane to shift the body's energetic patterns is a profound healing tool. Working on the spiritual plane is also the key for empowering attitudinal changes, shifts of consciousness that can effect positive personal and global change.

## Preparing to Heal with Shamanic Tools

These approaches are intuitive, not strategic. Many shamans simply apply the elements to connect their clients with the oneness of the natural world which restores the flow of energy throughout their body. Others bring light to areas that they perceive in the spiritual realm as dark. This increases the health and well-being of their clients. They don't intellectualize energy systems, but simply observe where the energy is stuck and work to free it. This isn't saying that there aren't those who conceptualize energy systems. Some indigenous groups, such as the Maya, have even mapped the flow of life force through the subtle circuits of the earth, our mother's energy body. We're also not implying that those employing strategies don't use their intuition. Of course, they do. Regardless, the following approaches are non-strategic with regard to releasing blocked energies. Shamans trust their intuition, the compassionate spirits and universal forces working through them. Reiki practitioners trust their intuition and the universal life force channeling through them. The Shamanic Reiki practitioner needs no road map, only an open heart.

Most Reiki practitioners experience expanded states, focused attention and increased awareness of bodily sensations when channeling Reiki energy. This is a great foundation for shamanic work, remarkably similar to mild shamanic trance or ecstatic states that heighten intuition. From here, the rest is simple, just open and become one with the energies flowing through you. What does becoming one with the energies mean? Did you ever as a young child play in a sandbox or go to the beach on a warm, sunny day? Try to recall the sensual aspects of that experience as if it were happening now. Imagine the sun heating your back as your hands sift through the warm grains of sand; with your mind and body completely relaxed, you are feeling and sensing. Your mind is in a state of focused attention, absorbing every detail of experience, completely immersed in the senses. Your hands move as one with the sand, one with its texture and temperature. You are the sand.

To further this analogy and highlight the ecstatic quality of this work, we call some of our shamanic tools, shamanic toys. Feathers, flowers, and other shamanic items such as rattles, drums and bells, certainly light up a child's eye. What could be more sacred than awakening our child-like qualities to benefit others? All you need to do is relax, open your senses and immerse in your experience as a child does. This opens your intuition and helps you to move as one with the spirit of your shamanic tools. Moving as one with them makes it easier for your tools to direct you. Then they're freed to create the optimal healing circumstances for your client. If this approach resonates with you, you may want to add the suggestions below to your healing basket. Or they may inspire you to discover new ways of using shamanic tools to release blocked energies.

**Using Drums and Rattles to Release Blocked Energies**
Drumming frees congested or blocked energies. It attunes one to the

rhythms of the universe and that of the spirits, plants, animals and the earth. Drumming brings oneness; it restores the proper flow of energy in our bodies and facilitates right relationship with our environment.

The modern world is re-discovering the ancient healing power of rhythm and vibration. Researchers tell us that gentle drumming alters brain wave patterns inducing a natural meditative state and deep relaxation. Stress-caused ailments are eased by the gentle beat of the frame drum which brings us back to ourselves, to the rhythm of our own heart beat, and the pulse of our blood flowing through our body. Drumming synchronizes mind and body and connects us to the earth. It cleanses our energy field and harmonizes the flow of energy through us. The drumbeat reconnects us to our soul.

After invoking the Reiki symbols at the beginning of a session, and spending a few minutes channeling Reiki energy to relax the person, some gentle drumming can have a powerful effect. Drumming can relax the body and emotions, settle the mind, and synchronize the breathing of practitioner with client, a healing in itself and great preparation for hands on work. Drumming will induce alpha and theta brain waves, heightening intuition and inducing a mild trance state. Clients can actively journey to the beat of the drum, to connect with what's healing for them, or simply open to the vibration resounding through their bones, fluids, organs, tissues, mind and emotions. The drumbeat restores vital, natural rhythms and breaks up stagnant energies.

We can open to, and become one with, the spirit of our drum. We may experience the spirit of the animal, whose hide forms the drum, or we may simply feel and become one with the earth and universal spirits the drum connects us to. When we attune to the spirit of our drum we may find that the drum directs its own beat, fast or slow, steady or irregular, even directing us to place the drum over specific parts of the body. We may intuit blockages in these areas, which the drumbeat works to release. It's important to remember that people can be sensitive to sound, so we beat the drum softly and especially lightly around the head and ears. As during hands-on work when we stay in areas that our Shamanic Reiki hands are drawn to, we'll also drum for as long as we're drawn and in the areas that call us. We follow spirit's nudge and hope you'll do the same. When you know the drum is finished, channeling Reiki energy to the places you've drummed will refine the healing process. Remember to hold off any discussion of what the client may have experienced during the drumming until after the Shamanic Reiki session is complete.

Although you may find the drum particularly good at dispersing stagnant energies, the rattle can be used in a similar way and can be especially good at locating blockages. When you intend for your rattle to be used for healing it will teach you how it wants to be used and what its healing gifts are. Rattles are made of various earth materials, such as sea grasses, gourds and animal skins filled with corn or stones. You may experience the rattle's energy as softer than the drum's, just see what you notice. We've experienced that rattles can be used to smooth areas where drums have dispersed energy, or they can be used alone to smooth out congested areas. See what your experience is. By listening to your heart and feeling spirit's nudge, you'll choose whether to use a drum or a rattle. And as drums and rattles have their own spirit, you'll start to recognize their call.

Some Siberian shamans sway their bodies back and forth in detecting energy blockages in their clients. The swaying cuts through discursive mind and opens body wisdom and earth/spirit connection so they can see their client's energy. You may want to try this as you rattle. Remember to approach this with the openness of a child's mind. Get out of your head and go into your bodily experience. Your body can be an extension of your shamanic tool, so you can feel where you need to rattle, as well as how to do so and when to move to a new location. Let yourself become one with the spirit of your rattle and it may shake softly and slowly in some areas and pick up speed in others. Don't intellectualize, just rattle over your client's body wherever you feel like rattling. Over time you'll experience increased oneness with your rattle and it'll teach you how best to work with it. The rattle can become a powerful and trustworthy tool. Notice when you feel drawn to drum or rattle during Shamanic Reiki sessions. Follow spirit's nudge. The drum or rattle can also be used to facilitate any shamanic journey the client takes.

**Releasing Blocks with Flowers, Stones and Plants**

Similar to what we experience during drumming or rattling, while moving our hands slowly over, or lightly touching our client, we may, for reasons we can't express, feel where the energy isn't flowing smoothly through part of the client's body. Instead of feeling the tug through our drum or rattle, we may detect this as an area that feels dense, congested, warm, cool or tingly upon our hands. Or there may be a clicking sensation in our hands. Any of these experiences can mean we're intuiting an energy blockage, although we also may have no physical sensations at all. Instead, we may simply know where blockages are, seeing or sensing them with our inner vision. Typically they're seen as dark areas. We can remain in an area and channel Reiki energy as it will loosen energy blocks, or we can use the shamanic techniques presented here.

When we locate such an area, we place one of our healing stones or crystals (black tourmaline works well) there and simply leave the stone in place. We charge the stone with whatever Reiki symbols feel appropriate as well as the intention that the stone will dissolve or suck out the blockage. If you are a Level One practitioner, charging the stone with intention is sufficient, then, forget about it while continuing the session. Or, we use two healing stones and click the stones together over the blocked area to dislodge the energies. This is similar to the way we vibrate our drum or rattle in these areas. In either scenario, we'll put our stones in the sea salt water when we're finished.

Many shamanic cultures in Peru, Ecuador and other Latin or South American areas consider carnations as especially good vehicles of spirit. Quechua Andean shamans tell us carnations magnetize the healing powers of sacred volcanoes. The usual flower colors are red, pink and white. To enlist the help of our flowers, we'll take two or three carnations from a vase that we've set up before the session. Holding them by the stem, we'll lightly tap the client on the part of the body where we've felt the blockage. After a few moments, we'll channel Reiki energy to the same spot. While doing so, we'll see or sense if the blockage is freed or loosened. If not, we'll try a second time. If the blockage is gone, we'll set the flowers aside and continue the session. After the session, we'll give our client the flowers (in a small paper bag) to bury in the earth. They can do so later that day or immediately following the session if the practitioner lives in a rural area. We'll invite them to thank the earth mother for the healing and ask her to absorb and transmute any energy trapped within the flowers, joining it with the universal energy stream. After burying the flowers, clients can burn the paper bag they were carried in within a fire pit or woodstove, or discard it in a paper recycling bin.

The energy of flowers is also particularly good for alleviating stress. If our client comes to the session angry or stressed, or we sense tension somewhere in their body, such as shoulders, arms or legs, we'll ask the flowers to alleviate that tension. We follow the same procedure as above, opening the session with the Reiki symbols and channeling the energy. Then we stop and use the flowers in the same way, lightly tapping them in the places where the client holds anger or stress. Or we can rest the flowers on one part of the body, asking that the energy become more relaxed there, as we place our hands to channel Reiki in other areas. This approach is especially valuable if stress or energy blockages appear in sensitive areas. In this case we'll give the client some flowers without stems. They'll connect with, and ask the flowers to help their healing and place them where they're drawn on their own body. Remarkably, people usually know exactly where the flowers want to go, even if it's the first time they've done this.

Other plants such as evergreen branches can absorb stress. If we sense tension on our client's back, for instance, we'll place the evergreen branch here and wipe the area like a sponge to sop up the tension. Or we'll place several healing stones there and invite the stones do the work while the client lays face down. We'll press slightly on each stone after we place them on the body, asking them to remove tension. If we later feel the tension isn't gone, we'll press the stones again slightly.

It's always preferable to include the client in their own healing, as this empowers them. This is one of the differences between Shamanic Reiki and Reiki. To support this, we may offer that they can visualize the energy blockage, tension, anger, or other emotion that's in a specific part of the body. We then place a rock or flower there, slap the flowers over it, or sponge it with an evergreen branch. We'll ask them to see or feel the tool acting like a magnet as we continue channeling Reiki energy. As the magnet pulls the stress out, they may want to visualize or feel what's within them as a solid block, like an intrusion. As the tool is used, for instance slapping flowers, we'll ask them to feel or see the flowers breaking up the block and pulling it up and out of them. Then we'll offer the same visualization that they had done earlier. We'll ask our clients to see light from the earth coming in and filling the area completely. They'll do this until either they or we sense the stress or energy blockage, or whatever we used the shamanic tool for is gone. This can also be done while using a drum or rattle. Just ask the person to visualize the vibrations of either the drum or rattle as arrows or darts, streaming from the drum or rattle, going into them, penetrating the solid block and continuing down into the earth. Each time an arrow passes through the block, ask the client to visualize it taking some of the blockage with it. This continues until the person let's us know the obstruction is completely gone. It will have recycled into universal energy.

We hope you understand the simplicity of this work. It's simply trusting that the earth and universal energy will benefit your client. If you don't have carnations you can use other kinds of flowers. If you don't have flowers but live near trees, you can ask a healthy tree to offer a few branches for healing purposes. Before cutting each branch, express gratitude and ask the tree to retract its energy just below the place you'll be cutting. You'll use them in the same way. Siberian Shamans from the Shor mountain region traditionally used birch tree branches for cleansings, and many Andeans use aromatic plants. Just make sure your assisting plants aren't poisonous, and you and the person you're working with aren't allergic to them. If you live in a city and can't cut tree branches, collect some sticks from the ground. Clean them physically and energetically and keep them in the house so you'll have them to use. You can tie some leaves around the stick before a session or use it alone. If you slap the client's body, just be sure to do it gently. Or roll the stick over the area, keeping your hands on the edges of the stick so the center of the stick rolls over the client's body. Never use a living tool such as flowers, leaves or sticks for more than one person. After the session, or at the end of the day, put the tools aside and return them to nature as described earlier.

**An Additional Visualization to Empower the Client**

If a person wishes to actively engage in their own healing, we can offer this additional guided visualization. It can be used to remove anything you or the client senses within them that no longer serves their higher good. You may use it with the shamanic tools spoken about in this chapter, or you may find that other shamanic tools nudge you to use it with them.

We start as in Chapter Two by visualizing a column of light originating from deep within the earth and rising up to our client. But in this visualization, the light enters them from the top of their head and moves in a clockwise direction, spiraling down through their body. When the light reaches the place where we've placed a flower or rock, we'll ask the person to see or feel this light gripping whatever's blocking its flow. We'll invite our client to imagine the light gently pushing the obstacle upward toward their skin and into the rock or flower. Then the light continues to spiral through their body. The person should experience a constant stream of light flowing into, through and out of them. Now their energy will be flowing as it should. If our client tells us the obstacle is resisting being moved into the tool, we'll remind them that this light is fueled and powered by the earth which is far more powerful than any blockage. After hearing this and reconnecting with the earth, they usually see the shamanic tool absorbing the obstacle, often sucking it up like a vacuum cleaner.

Used in the above ways, flowers, rocks, leafy branches and even sticks can help dissipate, move or remove whatever's obstructing the healthy flow of energy for people. We can also equally help our clients by using stones or flowers for different reasons and in different ways. For instance, we can apply stones with the intention of having them infuse our clients with energy, strength and power. We can do the same with flowers, brushing them over the face and body of a person, steeping them in the subtle healing qualities of the plant. Or, in intending both, barriers can be cleared while at the same time the person is saturated with the spirit and power of plant, stone or branch. This power will restore the client's energy flow and revive the person's relationship to the universal life force.

If you intuit another use for one or more of your shamanic tools to be helpful for your clients, trust that the tool will do whatever your intention guides.

# CHAPTER FIVE

# THE HEALING POWER OF THE ELEMENTS

As we said earlier, Reiki in its purest form is a marvelously simple modality. All that's required is the practitioner's intent to connect with the universal life force energy. From that point forward, the practitioner need do nothing but channel Reiki energy for healing. Reiki directs itself to where it's most called for in the client's body; relaxing, rejuvenating, dispersing congested energies, and bringing the client to a harmonious state. But by integrating shamanic perspectives with Reiki, the healing session becomes a wonderfully holistic experience that's tailored to each person.

As the Shamanic Reiki practitioner's trust in spirit deepens, it's easier to follow spirit's nudge and let the universe do most of the work. However, nearly every healer knows we can't leave everything to the universe; the universe demands that we participate with it. No matter how effective or even miraculous a healing session is in alleviating dis-ease, the symptoms that are usually the most obvious and later indicators of imbalance will return if we don't deal with their cause. Many times, the earlier and more subtle signals of dis-ease may have been ignored. You've been unhappy at your job for years but successfully suppressed your feelings as you're convinced you have no other options. Or you stay in an emotionally abusive relationship but deny anything's wrong because you're afraid to manage on your own. When we don't find a way to deal with, or we don't acknowledge, what's out of balance in our lives, it's not unusual for our bodies to tell us loudly that something's askew; symptoms can be such messages. To participate with the universe and to sustain our healing, we need to address the underlying issues that triggered our problems in the first place.

From a basic perspective, most people would interpret long-term healing benefit to mean that their problem has not only been cleared, but that it won't return. For this to occur, it's necessary for clients to shift their attitudes, behaviors, relationships and environments. Sometimes these changes happen easily since Reiki and shamanic work can shift root energetic causes of imbalances. In this case, similar to a domino effect, once core imbalances shift, destructive tendencies also shift allowing healthier patterns to spontaneously replace them. But it's more often the case that the deeper work to stay balanced starts once the person steps off the table.

An example of this is Dr Mikao Usui's commitment in the late 1800s to offer free Reiki treatments to beggars living on the streets of Kyoto, Japan. As the story goes, Usui did so with great success until seven years later when he started noticing some of these same folks back on the streets again, despite the healing and transformation they'd experienced. What happened was something many shamans understand concerning personal responsibility: people are more likely to transform when they're committed to, and involved with, their own healing process. Once Dr Usui understood why administering Reiki treatments alone weren't enough to ensure lasting change, he began empowering people to channel Reiki themselves.

Indigenous shamanic teachers, Ipupiara Makunaiman from the Ure-e-wau-wau tribe of Brazil and his Peruvian shaman wife, Cleicha Toscano, often say to their students, "All change comes from within." To ensure that the beneficial effects of a healing continue, clients must do the follow-up work. This work is best identified by the clients themselves, though it can be supported and guided by the healer. The first requirement for changing something from within is having the strongest intention to do so, we must deeply want it. Secondly, we have to be more conscious, to make new choices and let go of thoughts, emotions and actions that aren't helpful. It takes commitment and awareness to acknowledge what we're feeling and do something about it.

## Shamanic Life Tests

Alternately, some clients do have a miraculous healing leaving them symptom-free and they nourish change with healthier life patterns. Yet, the time will still arrive when old demons come back to haunt them or they'll feel tested beyond their limits. Change, initiating it and sustaining it, is notoriously difficult. Hundreds of groups exist throughout the world to support people wrestling with addictions and other problems, for that very reason.

Life has its challenges and there are times that truly test us, yet consciously navigating them ultimately brings strength. Most of us experience life not as a straight and narrow path, but as a bumpy and challenging adventure. Ours is a very human journey. Life's testing is about opening our hearts to be more compassionate and our minds to new directions, opportunities and aspects of ourselves. We're called to be fully present each step of the way and to remember our oneness, our connection to all things. Not until we do this can we embrace higher goals in life, or even understand that we have higher goals. This is especially important during these times of global change. In looking back, we often see that our most difficult times may have instigated the deepest growth. It's often clear only in retrospect that spirit nudged us exactly where we needed to go. Hindsight is always 100 percent correct.

Shamanic tests are always opportunities. But whether the opportunity is taken depends on how we perceive it and what we do with it. Regardless of advice, past or present teachings, education or intelligence, and even our willingness to change our life's direction, our responses are often habitual and not in our best interest. If you ask a person trying to lose weight how easy it is to translate their intentions into action, most will tell you it's not. We've said before that more time is needed for each client than the fifty-minute hour. But your clients can't call you numerous times during the day for the support they need to navigate life's challenges. Our task is to help people do the work they need to do once they leave our healing space, live more consciously and embrace shamanic tests as opportunities. In these ways they can fulfill their highest potential and benefit the world.

Once Mikao Usui saw personal responsibility as the necessary ingredient for lasting transformation, he began teaching and attuning people to do Reiki. As Shamanic Reiki practitioners we can follow Dr Usui's example to teach as well as heal, by introducing our clients to shamanic friends they can call on whenever needed. The relationship established with these new shamanic friends can heal, balance, and help people access inner guidance when most needed. This empowers them to stay on a healing path long after the session is over, without depending on the healer who helped discern that path.

**Concept**

Ancient shamanic cultures saw everything that existed in this world as belonging to one of the main elements – earth, air, fire, water and space or ether. In the shamanic worldview, each element has spiritual qualities that can be accessed through the shamanic journey or simply by consciously directing our awareness to it. On the simplest level, each of these elements has its own unique physical properties and energetic attributes, though all arise from the same primordial source. By invoking and merging with the elements, that is, consciously connecting with them and experiencing their material traits as well as their subtle and energetic characteristics, we can more intimately know and support ourselves since we are made of these same elements.

The shamanic allies we invite you to introduce to your clients are the spiritual qualities of the elements. When you and your clients develop a personal relationship with these elements you open the door for healing and magic to occur.

Most everyone today is aware of how healing it can be to spend time in nature. Take a moment right now to remember how you've felt after a long hike in a beautiful forest, after swimming in a pristine lake, when watching a glorious sunset, or in listening to a morning cacophony of spring birds. Remember what your body felt like, what you experienced emotionally or mentally. Chances are that even if you weren't relaxed to begin with, in noticing and feeling the wonder of the world around you after being with nature for even a few moments, you began to feel peaceful. When we immerse in the elements, we feel synchronized and balanced; we feel good in a basic way. Being in nature reconnects us to the sacred flow of life, and our inseparability with all things. The survival of our species depends on this awareness now more than ever.

The earth body is not separate from our own skin, ligaments and bones. Our internal waters are one with the oceans, lakes and rivers. Our digestive and cellular heat is inseparable from the fire of the sun, volcanoes and stars. The winds that can cleanse and energize our planet can also purify and revitalize us with every breath we take. The vast space of the sky and the heavens, the space that holds the potential for what's physical and material, is the same space that rests between our words and thoughts and the gaps between our breaths. It is one and the same with the vast internal spaces in our bodies and cells, and the space of human consciousness itself.

Remembering our oneness with the elements rejuvenates our bodies, shifts our consciousness and nurtures our souls. It connects us to what's sacred and helps us change in ways that change our world.

## Developing a Personal Approach

Earlier, we mentioned the simplicity of shamanism. This is an important point. We've also mentioned that the most powerful shamans we've met are those who glean directly from nature and spirit – and we believe the only true shamanic teachers are the spirits themselves. Human teachers can point us in the right direction and facilitate relationships with shamanic animal guides, teachers, spirits and energies that interface physical reality. But in looking at the diverse ways shamanism is approached and practiced around the world, it's easy to see there aren't any hard and fast rules. If it works for you, it works. This is extremely important. The new shamanic practitioner may ask how to forge a bond with the elements – for instance, which attributes of water best facilitate healing and change. We could answer, churning, destructive, flexible, fluid, furious, gentle, grinding, powerful and soothing, for starters, but our answers may not be the experience you need. The invitation is for you and your clients to bond with each element in whatever way works for you. Your own discovery will match your needs much more precisely than anything we could tell you. And uncovering these on your own will deepen your relationship to each element you engage.

Therefore, we won't go to great lengths to describe each element as you can ascertain their qualities on your own. Instead, we'll offer some guidance and head you in the right direction so you can begin your own relationship and feel confident to help clients begin theirs. If you don't already have a rapport with the elements, be sure to connect with them first before introducing these friends to those you work with. The more personally we experience nature's capacity to heal, energize, offer wisdom and reflect our true nature, the easier it is to guide others to seek them out. That's the goal of this chapter, to facilitate your client's active engagement with the elements for a deeper relationship to themselves and the world. In the shamanic world, everything is about relationship. The more we explore and interact with nature, the elements, and our shamanic tools and guides, the more intimate and trustworthy these relationships become.

**A Word on Journeying**

In the last few chapters, you've been reading about how to use empowering imaginative journeys with your clients, and by now you should be familiar with the process. It's not difficult. As we've said before, going into the spirit reality is nothing more than closing your eyes or relaxing and expanding your attention to daydream that you're there. Many approaches are included below which you might want to add to your healing basket. Several of these are founded on the journeying method, so open your senses and let your imagination fly. Again, you and your clients shouldn't worry if you're not seeing with your inner vision; simply open to feeling and experiencing in whatever way presents itself to you. With time and practice, you'll feel comfortable journeying and be able to enter the alternate reality at will.

**Cleansing with the Elements**

Though it helps to be in nature when you connect with the elements, it's not necessary because everything is comprised of the elements; we can open to them even while sitting in our living room.

An easy way to initiate a relationship with the elements is with an exercise John Perkins introduces at shamanic workshops, called *Cleansing with the Elements*. *Cleansing with the Elements* is something you and your client can do at anytime, even if you're sitting on a busy subway or bus, but please don't journey if you're in the driver's seat. You can introduce this practice to clients when they come to your healing space and after that they can try it on their own.

Your client can journey to the elements anytime during the session, but doing so at the beginning helps them relax and go more deeply into the work that follows. If including *Cleansing with the Elements* within the hands-on part of the session, we begin as we usually do, and as soon as we feel the person's breathing relax and the tension of the day seemingly dissipate, we invite them to take this journey through their active imagining. If introducing this practice before the hands-on part of the session begins, we'll instruct our clients in it and *Cleanse with the Elements* together as we sit across from each other in meditation.

As with all the approaches we've introduced, you're the best one to determine how to apply this in your own practice. Remember that this exercise also stands on its own as a powerful ally. Your client can now go home and access the power of the elements at any time to feel renewed and strengthened whenever needed.

Before they journey, we explain to people that they're to simply allow the elements to release and cleanse whatever tensions, worries and stresses they've come to the session with. We suggest that in the journey space, they actively imagine and experience, in whatever way is right for them, the elements coming to heal and renew them. Usually when asked which of the elements they're most drawn to, regardless of shamanic background, most people will immediately answer. Clients can begin by calling on that element, yet if not sure which, they can ask for the element most currently needed to come to them first.

Remember that we've spoken about the spirits being the true teachers. Though we suggest beginning with one element, the elements often have their own agenda. They may come to us one after the other in any order, or several may appear at once. If that happens there's no need to push the other elements away, but rather relax and enjoy whichever of them emerge. The elements aren't ultimately separate from each other anyway, and the goal is to feel their power infusing us in whatever way this happens. We don't need to understand why water is doing what it's doing, all we need is to experience is the water in our journey and feel its energy. When getting a massage, most of us try not to spend too much time wondering why the massage therapist is kneading our shoulders. It's more important to go into the experience, to feel it. We also surrender to how it feels to have the elements working on us, instead of analyzing what they're doing. This is not an intellectual exercise as it's designed to involve us more deeply than this. We can always dissect and intellectualize later.

The range of feelings and emotions that clients may experience as the elements cleanse them are limitless. They may feel as if they're rolling in mud that cleanses them to their core. They may imagine themselves flying on an eagle's back through heavy winds that blow their tension and worries away. They may sense they're being immersed in a clear pool of water with a waterfall cascading down upon them washing and renewing every cell of their being. Flames burning off obstacles may engulf clients. They may be lying on a sandy beach as the warm sun soothes and nurtures them, after which waves gently roll over them carrying away what the sun has loosened from their body, emotions and mind. They may experience being suspended in the vastness of space, feeling expanded, nourished and limitless.

Or none of this may happen and the elements may come as different forms altogether, as animals, spirit guides, sacred symbols or objects. It is the spirit of the element that heals, and the form through which they present themselves is changeable. What's important is to experience and trust that whatever happens is what's meant to happen. It's good to take as much time as needed or wanted for this exercise.

We ask our clients to whisper to us when the journey's finished, and we invite them to take a moment to notice how they feel, sharing with us whatever they'd like about the experience. This knowledge may guide us throughout the session so that we can support the work the elements have begun.

It's important to know that you can *Cleanse with the Elements* at any time and though each time will be different, it will be just as powerful and effective. When we open to the elements, we heal our separation from nature and open to the sacred world that interfaces material reality.

A more fundamental approach to developing a relationship with the elements is to learn to merge with them, and in doing so, deepen our connection to each element. This opens the door for us to experience and make available these intrinsic qualities in ourselves. It's also the first step we take to consciously apply specific properties of the elements to support our healing path. We often give our clients the assignment of connecting with nature, which is great for ongoing work, but also valuable for those coming for just one session. A relationship with the elements will support us for a lifetime.

The following section can be explored by clients independently or can be integrated into the Shamanic Reiki session. It's especially advantageous to go outside and do these practices with clients the first time they try it – this obviously works best if you're scheduling longer appointment times. But it's good to know that this approach can also be used exclusively in the journey space while actively imagining. If introducing it in this way during hands-on work, it's important to be well into the Shamanic Reiki session before guiding people on their journey. We'll leave it to you to alter the directions to fit the journey format.

**Merging with the Spirit of the Elements**
What are the concrete elemental characteristics of our world? There are tall majestic mountains, blue skies, fertile valleys, volcanoes, starry nights, forests, both new and old, rivers, fierce and gentle winds, and oceans to name a few. There are huge boulders and vast expanses of night sky. There are tall, jagged cliffs towering over white-capped wind-whipped seas, and gentle meadows sloping down to touch lakes or rivers. And just as important, there are barren wastelands of ice and frozen

ground, deserts where not even animals or plants exist, and areas where mud may boil and bubbles of sulfur pop into the sky. All these, both beautiful and harsh, are part of our world and each part has a spirit. But what does the spirit of each place feel like? And what attributes, strengths and healing properties do merging with these energies offer us? By attuning and using shamanic methods, we can find out.

Living in an area where we can walk out on the land is ideal and being barefoot is the optimal way to first feel our connection with the earth. As we walk, we open our heart and awareness to feel each step and movement of our bodies. We awaken all five of our senses to the elements around us feeling the breezes, temperatures, listening to the sounds, experiencing the smells and tastes, and noticing what we see. We also open to more subtle sensations and perceptions, letting go of mundane thoughts so we can take in the full wonder of nature. We walk to where we're drawn and invite a connection with the spirit of the place. To do this, we simply rest our minds, open our hearts and ask permission to be there. (Don't forget that this can be done in our reality or in the spiritual one of the shamanic journey.)

Tuvans, as is true of shamans the world over, are intimately attuned to the elements. They live and walk lightly upon the earth, represented by the upturned toes of their traditional yak fur boots. When traveling across vast expanses of steppe, mountains and taiga (Siberian evergreen forests), Tuvan shamans are known to honor the spirits of the rivers, trees, winds and land by making offerings, prostrating upon the earth and doing ceremony.

We can also commune with these spirits, expressing our gratitude and feeling our oneness with them. The spirits of the place may commune back with us, even offering a symbol or message that we perceive intuitively, many times providing just the medicine we need at this time in our lives. When we arrive at the place we're drawn to, we can make a simple offering, such as to kneel on the ground and place our palms and forehead down to the earth as some Tuvans do. Or we can find a tree that calls us and place our palms and forehead against the tree. As we do so, we relax our mind and body, open our heart and feel our gratitude. We take our time, as long as we're drawn, simply being in this way. The spirit of the place may come to us with a message, or simply fill us with energy and love.

Later, when we thoroughly feel one with the place (something that may seem more challenging for city dwellers, but is just as possible), we may be drawn to bend down and pick up a stone. By now, we're feeling completely at ease in our environment and cast our awareness outward to the rock in our hand. Or we may be drawn to doing so with the flowers we smell, the wind swaying the branches of a tree near us, the sparkling stream below us or expanse of blue sky above us. As we gaze at what draws our attention, we relax our vision and our minds, immersing in the experience. We allow ourselves to enter the stream, wind, rock, or whatever we gaze upon with our full awareness. We permit ourselves to become one with what we gaze upon as we did when feeling our oneness with the spirit of the place. We may feel our physical body becoming the rock, flowers or stream, but the item itself is not as important as the connection we've made to its spirit.

There's no better way to feel the power of the elements, and our own power, than by experiencing oneness with nature. Whenever we feel tense, worried, ill, or otherwise imbalanced, we can immerse in nature to rejuvenate and restore our energy. Ancient peoples knew and tapped the energies of the mythological reality that paralleled the physical reality for healing, guidance and sustenance. They were the original planetary stewards who knew that care, gratitude and reverence opened the door to nature's forces and magical realms. They knew that living in balance with, and being awed by the beauty of streams, trees, breezes, stars and other natural entities encouraged them to respond. We can do the same. By simply opening to, appreciating, and lying down upon the earth, for example, we can be renewed and strengthened. We can actively breathe this earth energy into us, circulating renewal and strength with our breath throughout our body, mind and emotions. By feeling our oneness with the trees, being touched by their beauty and speaking freely to them about our challenges and problems, we may spontaneously find resolve for what's troubling us. By attuning to and having reverence for the element of fire, as Quechua Andean shamans do with sacred volcanoes, we can empower wishes and goals. If we live rurally we can create a small fire pit in our back yard to meet the element of fire. If not, candles or a fireplace will do. We can sit silently by waters, streams, oceans, rivers and lakes attuning to their energies, feeling one with and healed by them. And even if we can't leave our house, we can merge with the wind for instance, by sitting in front of a fan or by an open window.

As we attune to nature and merge with the elements, life becomes more dynamic and intimate. Experiencing our oneness heals our bodies, expands our consciousness and gives us fresh ways to look at our world and ourselves. These ways, these new insights, will be unique for each of us.

The elements are always available to us wherever we are. It may be easier to feel our oneness directly in nature, but merging with the elements within the journey state is just as valid. We need only to open to them with gratitude and reverence to unlock their magic and power. And since the elements give to us so generously, let's begin to understand our own profound responsibility as earth's stewards, just as our shamanic ancestors did ages ago.

**Communicating with the Elements**
When we feel connected and have experienced our oneness with the elements, another approach is to actively communicate with the stone, tree, stars, or other entity, asking about specific physical and spiritual qualities that may help us. We'll do this in a similar way, but in the journey space. The first step, again, is to simply open, relaxing mind, body and emotions and feeling our gratitude. When we're at harmony with the element we're sensing, we'll cast our awareness into the stone, tree or star or whatever it is. We'll take our time and open to the communication happening in any way, through vision, knowing, felt sense, words, symbols, color, or emotion. The elements communicate to us in myriad ways depending on circumstance and personal orientation, so having patience and attuning to subtlety is essential. Soon, we'll be able to sense what specific qualities the element suggests we can bring into our

life to help us on our healing journey.

We recognize that life isn't that simple and it's important to know that what people come back with after such journeys isn't always easy to navigate. This isn't a problem, just an opportunity to trust that inner voice, your own, or spirit's whispering, so that what needs to be said comes naturally and you'll be helpful to the people you work with.

For example, qualities revealed when mountains are journeyed to may be volcanic, tall, majestic, steadfast, destructive, immovable and tenacious. It's important for clients and healers not to judge the qualities perceived. Volcanic eruptions such as Mount St Helens can completely destroy everything in their path, a show of force telling everyone that nothing can withstand the power of nature. But full and rich plant and animal life have returned to that mountain because, after all, destruction is an intrinsic quality of volcanoes and nature, all in the cycle of death that makes way for new life. In nature there's no good or bad trait, simply what is. All is part of the whole. These traits aren't good or bad for us either, but can benefit us when consciously applied. Destruction, for instance, can be an important energy, just the right energy for cutting through stubborn habitual patterns.

No matter what attributes people access in their journeys to the elements, they can be interpreted in many ways, and it can be helpful for your clients to explore with you how to apply these attributes for their own benefit. When committed to changing, people will usually interpret their journeys in ways that advance their healing and reduce destructive behavior, as opposed to reinforcing old negative patterns. The client who has a quick temper and gives in to road rage, for example, must first notice what they're feeling and then choose to enlist the help of the elements. They may think of a briskly flowing stream whose cool qualities cool their anger and ask its energy to help the anger flow through and out of them as if carried by a swiftly moving stream. A person who allows others to control them may commit to noticing just when they're about to give in to demands that aren't in their best interest simply because they've always done it. When they do make this commitment, they may draw on more evocative water qualities to be more assertive.

Summoning tidal currents or crashing waves can abruptly wash away hesitancy and imbue them with the power to deal with challenges that arise when taking a new stand.

Don't be disappointed if it doesn't happen this easily, it rarely does. But having a personal relationship with the spirit of the elements opens the door to a myriad of attributes we can call upon to shift out of habitual patterns.

If our clients can't walk in nature, or even in parks, to make a connection with the elements, they can sit quietly in their homes. They can hold a stone or twig, place their hands in a bowl of sea-salt, gaze at a photograph of a mountain or prairie, touch or smell the soil of a plant or plant stalk or flower, look out the window to trees or sky, or simply close their eyes and travel by memory to their favorite place in nature or allow their imagination to take them where it will. From there, the journey begins and what comes will be just as valid. And as mentioned earlier, you can also guide your people to journey to the elements during their Shamanic Reiki session. Or, you can go outside with them to introduce these approaches if your healing space is rural (you can do this in the city, too).

Wherever you or your clients begin, it's important to journey to each element several times, asking them about their helpful attributes. Again, these attributes may be double edged. But healing progresses more rapidly when we employ the help of our shamanic allies and we can trust that whatever the elements show us is a helpful trait, one that we likely can very much use. There's no further guidance needed. Your relationship will be shaped by the qualities of nature that are found where you live, travel to and through what your imagination reveals.

### Empowering and Transmuting with Fire

Fire focuses and activates higher intentions, cleanses the energy field, and is the prime transformer used for millennia by indigenous people to shift the form of matter. Fire can burn away obstacles and unhealthy patterns, and shine the light on and empower deeper wishes. We've mentioned that longer sessions offer more opportunity to empower clients once they leave our healing space. *Cleansing with the Elements* and taking people either on journeys, or directly out into nature to connect with the elements are two ways to expand a healing session into an empowering retreat. *Empowering and Transmuting with Fire* is another. All are practices your client can continue long after they arrive home. You may add this exercise to your healing basket or change and expand it in whatever ways you're inspired. You may also choose to employ the other elements, instead of fire, in a similar way.

If we're inviting our clients to *Cleanse with the Elements* when sitting with us in meditation, we'll complete that exercise before initiating the practice presented here. Then, to start, we'll ask our clients to contemplate a few things, such as, what their highest wish is for themselves, and who they aspire to be. We ask if they are aware of what they want to change and what they want to empower in their lives and what their heart and soul long for.

After clients have had a few silent moments to consider these questions, we'll then invite them to hold an unlit white candle while they close their eyes and connect in the journey space with the element of fire which the candle represents. This connection has been aided by their experiences of fire in *Cleansing with the Elements*, although in this case we're not inviting our clients to journey with or to fire, but to simply feel their connection to the power of this element in whatever way comes to them.

Once this connection is established, we'll invite a second, more focused meditation, this time on the wishes they just reflected on. First, our clients should clearly see these goals, at the same time feeling in their bodies as if these were true in their lives right now. What would it feel like if these aspirations were reality now? We ask them to make this experience as real as they can. As they do this we encourage our clients to also speak these aspirations aloud if they're drawn. We, as practitioners and sacred witnesses hold a loving, unconditional space. We also invite the person to speak out loud anything they become aware of that may hold them back from their wishes.

Then we'll ask our clients to blow or *camay* their wishes three times into the unlit white candle while really feeling what they want in their lives as they do this, infusing and mixing these intentions with the trans-mutational energy of fire. As mentioned in Chapter Four, shamans the world over camay, blow with the breath of spirit. Camaying, a Quechua word, transmits consciously directed spiritual energy. It is the same act a Reiki master employs when blowing the Reiki symbols into the energy field of the person being attuned to Reiki.

We'll then place the unlit candle under the Shamanic Reiki table during the session and explain to our clients that their intent and what they have voiced, felt and infused into the element of fire (the potential that the unlit candle represents), will be reinforced during the session.

When our clients return home, we ask them to light the candle for the first time and to meditate while sitting in front of the burning flame. They should do a similar mediation in front of the lit candle three nights in a row. For the first two nights they ask the fire to help them focus on what they want to bring to their life. They again feel these wishes in their bodies, emotions and minds as if they were already true. Then they blow or snuff the candle out. On the third night they ask the fire to help them see what they need to magnetize, what they need to concretely achieve or bring to their lives to make these wishes reality. The fire may also show them what they need to change, what they need to let go of, to shift or act upon, to reach their goals and become who they want. As our clients do so on this third night, they ask the fire to strengthen within them the power to transmute their own lives while they let the candle burn completely down. It's during this time, while the candle burns, that people can empower their commitment to heal and act on the information they've received from the elements. They can envision themselves doing so over the next weeks, months and years, in order to create the life that they want to live. If possible, we'll also suggest that our clients make a simple offering of bread, loose tobacco or flower petals to the earth and to the element of fire in gratitude for what's been received. We invite you to do the same.

When a person seeks spirit's help, they can learn to help themselves in subtle, yet profound ways, such as cleansing or merging with the power of the elements for guidance, healing and strength, and accessing elemental qualities to serve any moment's needs or to empower new goals and life directions. Calling on the wisdom of the elements is an empowering act that reflects personal responsibility and a willingness to change. All that's required beyond this is an open heart, and the elements will always respond.

# CHAPTER SIX

# SHIFTING THE ENERGY OF
# PAST EVENTS

Time doesn't exist in shamanic realms as we experience it in our reality. We regard time as linear, with any given moment having a fixed place on a time continuum that began as a defined past, advanced to the present, and will propel forward into what we perceive as the future. From a linear paradigm, it's logical to believe that once something occurs, its place on the time continuum is forever fixed. But have you ever wished you could go back in time to change something you did or erase something you said? And have you ever wished that a past event still affecting you now simply never happened?

From a linear point of reference, wishing such things is fantasy. But in shamanic reality this isn't exactly the case. Because shamans view time differently, they can journey to a past event which still impacts the present and help release energetic ties from this time period. Clients can also embark on an empowering healing journey themselves if that feels more warranted. However we shift our connection to past events, upon returning to ordinary reality, the event has still occurred. Yet the energy and associations with the events can be altered.

In Chapter Three we shared the concept of energetic attachments and how to remove them. The unhealthy attachments that bind people remain with them until the mutual resonance keeping them in place shifts, either by acting and responding differently, or by removing them shamanically. Energetic cords transcend time and space. Regardless of when they origi-nated or whether the person the cords were created with is dead or alive, living in the same city or across the world, energetic attachments continue affecting those to whom they're attached.

Similarly, when something impacts us we can become attached to that event through the emotional reactions it elicits. Given a similar set of circumstances, past emotional responses may be triggered. A person bitten by a dog as a child may, as an adult, feel uncomfortable around dogs. Not everyone would consider this a problem. However, if circumstances required someone to be near dogs, such as a job, a new relationship with a person who owns a canine, a love of walking or jogging that exposes them to neighborhood dogs, a benign aversion could turn into a major issue. We can't return to the past to prevent the child from being bitten, but Shamanic Reiki can help free up the constriction caused by past events.

## Concept

By returning to a past event, we can alter the energy associated with it. This helps us respond in more empowering ways when similar events occur in the present. Someone willing to overcome a fear of dogs usually does so exclusively in the present, forgetting their fear is charged by the past. The problem can be addressed in the present by dealing with current behavior, or we can resolve its root causes through shamanic means. Just as Reiki energy can be sent into the past or future through intent and by utilizing symbols that surpass time and space, energy created by people and circumstances transcends linear boundaries. Going back in time we can disconnect the energy, not just in the present where we feel and observe its effect, but from the past that fuels it. This way, not only is the energy thwarted in current circumstances, it's halted at its source.

Regarding the example above, this doesn't mean that someone who's been fearful of canines will go out and buy a dog. Yet if past energy is disconnected and the energetic trauma of being bitten is freed, the person may have an easier time being around dogs. In the last chapter we mentioned that change can sometimes come immediately and with great ease. We also emphasized that in most instances, change demands time, effort, and a sincere desire to make things different. Given this, shamanic approaches offer expedient ways people can address issues that limit them.

## Preparing to Journey to the Past

It's impossible to cover the hundreds of reasons why a person would journey into the past to alter the energy affecting them. Shamanic Reiki practitioners follow intuition in deciding when, with which clients, and under what circumstances it's most helpful to do so.

Changing the energy charge of the past requires preparation before the hands-on part of a Shamanic Reiki session begins. This is another reason why longer appointment times offer optimal healing opportunities. If there's an indication that something from a person's past is hindering healthier expression, we'll explain about shifting energy attachments for a swifter, smoother healing. We explore whether the person is interested, prepared and committed to letting go of what's holding them back. The more traumatic the event, the more difficult the journey and the more preparation and post-work is needed.

We'll need to know our client's perceptions of the event and where it happened. Reiki Level Two practitioners and above will be able to send Reiki energy back to this time to help alter the energy. A Level One practitioner would simply place their Reiki hands over the client's heart and forehead. Reiki supports the client however the person's higher self directs and sends healing energy to the event our client is journeying to.

Feel free to alter the format presented, tailoring it to your situation and client. Before the hands-on part of the session, we ask people to imagine traveling back to the time and place where the event has occurred. The objective is for them to be a third party witnessing the event from above, just as they hovered over their bodies when looking for energetic attachments. As challenging as this may appear, no matter how traumatic the event was, the person should stay detached as if a spectator to the event. Processing emotionally is not the point of this practice. If you or your client feels this might be too difficult, offer that they instead travel back to the time just after the event occurred.

## Dialoguing with the Past Self

Earlier, we spoke of clients removing attachments by communicating with the higher self of the person who attached them. The next step we suggest to those we work with is similar. We invite them to dialogue with their past self just after the event occurred, regardless of the physical state they were in when it happened. In this communication our clients introduce themselves. This imaginative conversation takes place silently, as if a meeting of minds between two separate people. In essence, it is two people in one. One person is the one lying on the table before us and the other person is the client of the past, experiencing the past event. The person from the past will have no idea who the client of the present is or why they've suddenly appeared. The person we're working with must explain to the former self who they are, and that they've come from a future time to help overcome the energetic attachment associated with the event.

The main difference between the two people is that the one fixed in the past is looking ahead to a future which may appear bleak because of what's just transpired. The other, the client on the table, is glimpsing the past and how life has evolved since. As the former uses foresight to guess at a future strongly colored by immediate experience they'll perceive what's ahead through the lenses of a painful circumstance. The latter uses hindsight as they know how life continued following the trauma.

We'll also ask clients to silently verbalize within their journey to their past selves why it's important for both of them to heal this time just after the event has occurred. Using the example of the person bitten by the dog, the person will describe the future to their past selves. They may console this aspect of themselves and emphasize the positive and healthy things that will happen when they move on from this painful time.

Clients begin by expressing the reason they're journeying: "From today on, unless we change the way we feel, we'll always be afraid of dogs." It's then helpful to mention whatever good things have happened since that day long ago, "But 15 years from now we'll discover a new and wonderful career," or, "We'll meet the person we've been looking for." (They'll explain the reasons they'll want to overcome their fear of dogs at that future time.) "But we'll hesitate in that relationship because the person we're interested in will own and love several dogs, yet we'll still be afraid of them." We encourage people to use the pronoun *we* to remember that the conversation is between two aspects of themselves. The goal is for both past and present selves to observe what happened in the past as an event to move on from, in order to live a healthier present. Moving on doesn't minimize the impact of what occurred. Rather, this exercise helps people free whatever part of them is still attached to the past energy. The dog did attack the child, the husband or wife did die in the car accident, the fire did destroy the home and the client did lose everything. These are terrible things. But in addition to whatever work they've done to experience, process and clear the pain of these events, it's helpful to gain a time-oriented perspective. In this way clients see what they still cling to and what holds them back.

The most important thing the present self attempts to show the past self is that though terrible, the event was one of many in life and the future will progress for the better. The present self speaking to the past self knows this. They'll laugh again at some point and enjoy life once more. They'll survive this, the world hasn't ended. It's productive to give the past self as many concrete examples of future enjoyment as possible.

**More about Shifting the Past**

The person of the past is the energy source attached to the person of the present. From that energy arises the limiting responses associated with the event, such as a continued fear of dogs. In easing the claustrophobia a past self experiences, the person of the present can see from the larger perspective and into the future. They understand that unless the attachment releases, its energy may always limit them. Ideally, they will fervently wish to assist their past self in loosening the energetic attachment to the event as it's happening for them.

Getting the past self to reduce anxiety associated with the event isn't the same as going into a hospital and telling a car accident victim who has just lost his wife that everything will be fine. But ten years from that moment, the husband may be remarried and in moving on with his life find he's held back from giving himself fully to his new partner. Through shamanic journeying he can go back in time to the hospital and tell his younger self that life will go on. He expresses that he'll be happy again and that it's time for the past self to release the attachment to the event, even though for that past self, the event has just occurred. In the shamanic journey space, the trauma of the accident will soften because the man of the past lying on the stretcher will now know there's something more to live for. The man of the present will know it's true because for him, that future has already happened.

Using some of the examples noted above, clients may now feel more comfortable around canines or share more intimately with their partner. Without the negative tug from the past, people usually become more flexible.

## What to do in the Session

After preparing as described above, begin by channeling Reiki as in any Shamanic Reiki session. Rest your hands on the person, open and relax with the intention of having the life force energy flow through you to your client. When the person appears totally relaxed whisper that this is a good time to take the imaginative journey into the past time you both discussed. Unless otherwise guided, continue resting your hands lightly in the same place on the body. Aside from sending Reiki, our touch supports and grounds clients, especially when taking difficult journeys.

Those beyond Reiki Level One can invoke the long distance healing symbol and send Reiki back into the past. It can be sent to the client of the past just as the event occurred to decrease the traumatic effects. Clients will receive this energy in the present, helping them relax and open to the journey, as well as in the past, helping while the event is occurring. A Level One practitioner can simply place one hand near the person's heart and the other on their forehead, or check in to see what's comfortable for the client.

If the person you're working with is open to speaking during their imaginative journey back in time, they can keep you abreast of what's happening. You can offer gentle words of encouragement, suggestions to help calm the past self and help them conclude the journey successfully. You can direct Reiki back in time by following the client's lead with regard to what's happening. If the person says the child is crying because the dog just bit him in the leg, you may be guided to place your Reiki hands on your client's leg. In doing so, you can intend the energy to travel back to the past person's leg.

When the person indicates they've finished the journey, we continue sending Reiki to their heart for a few moments or wherever else we're drawn. If they've shed some tears, we may wipe their face with a tissue then place our hands on their cheeks sending Reiki there, as well. Follow your heart and let your intuition guide you. Most important is to be gentle and supportive. Along with channeling energy, sending love, warmth and well-being supports a smooth transition back into the present moment. We whisper to the person letting them know that in their own time and pace, they should slowly return to the room. After fully returning they can open their eyes when they feel ready. We make eye contact and speak with the person for a moment to make sure they're fully present. We then ask them to close their eyes again while we continue the Reiki session.

### How to Close the Session

It's important to have enough time at the end of such a session for clients to share their journey. The person may look to you for some direction as to where they go from here. Based on the journey you've supported them through, what you both discuss after the hands-on part of the session is over, and what intuitive insights you gain in the process, you'll have something helpful to offer.

It's also valuable to remember that some people aren't used to taking the proper time and space to allow experiences and emotions to settle. Given this, we'll invite clients to sit with us in silence for a while before speaking so they can connect with the full texture of what's occurred for them. How does their body feel, what emotions are bubbling up, what's their state of mind? We ask them to take some nice, deep cleansing breaths and to simply *be* with what they're experiencing for a few moments. We suggest they not rush quickly into answers, solutions and plans of action, but let the power of the journey percolate and sift through them first. Given a little time and space, experiences integrate in ways appropriate to each person. The next few days offer a rich time when additional insights may arise and/or cleansings may occur on emotional or physical levels. We support these opportunities by reminding people to drink lots of pure, fresh water, eat healthy foods, and to take reflective time. They can keep a journal, pay attention to dreams and synchronicities, and notice what they feel in the days following a session.

Clients may need the extra time to feel grounded before they leave your healing space. Having them drink a glass of water, making sure they make eye contact and suggesting they take a walk before getting into their car to drive home, are all good ways to help them synchronize. It's wise to end any session this way and particularly called for when doing more in-depth work. It can be helpful to schedule another session within a few days and it's important that your clients know they can reach you if needed. Make sure they have a support network of friends and family to call on if needed and if it appears they'll need a great deal of support, check in with them by phone that evening. Everything depends on the nature of the event and how quickly the person integrates the work. Shamanic Reiki combines channeling Reiki energy with past-self journeying, so a rapid and smooth integration is typical.

The event doesn't have to be major to be traumatic. An illustration is a person who, as a teenager, was traumatized at a dance when made fun of by several other teens. Though something like this can't claim the same level of importance as the death of a parent or spouse, and many of us wouldn't think its effects could be long lasting, it would never come up if not a source of angst. Regardless of how we perceive the intensity of the situation, the procedure of going back into the past is the same. Under less heavy circumstances, however, there may not be such a need for follow-up or to schedule successive sessions. It's also helpful to know that shifting the energy of isolated past incidents can positively impact other similar scenarios the person isn't journeying back to. Because of this, shifting shame felt from being ridiculed at a dance may have broad effect; it may help the person let go of more generalized self-esteem issues.

**Final Thoughts to Consider**
The first time you consider attempting this practice you may doubt

whether it's warranted. Trust your instincts and what arises in speaking with your client. Trust your intuition and follow your heart. Remember your message to spirit, your intention, is to do whatever's needed for the highest good of the person you're working with. With that as your priority, trusting yourself in relationship to your client's needs, inclinations and circumstances won't lead you astray.

It's also wise to stay open in the event that the unexpected occurs for people as they journey back into their past. You've got the message by now that spirit has its own agenda. When journeying to a past event, spirit may suddenly arrive on the scene to assist in releasing a limiting attachment to the past. It's not unusual, for instance, for the person of the present to observe a spirit guide or angel comforting their past self at the scene of a tragedy, despite the fact that this isn't something they recall experiencing at the time. Usually, but not always, the type of guide that appears is consistent with the person's spiritual orientation.

Having clear intention to remove the charge of an event puts the call out to spirit. Spirit will respond and may indeed convince you that it was an active agent all the time. The appearance of these spirit presences is consoling and can transform a person's relationship to what happened. The love and support they feel from these beings often stays with them long after they journey back into the present. It's reassuring, and can transform our perception and experience of what happens to us, to realize that in the midst of painful circumstances, spirit was right there with us.

When engaging *Past Shifting* with clients, don't forget the notion of shamanic tests from the last chapter. Many things occur over which we have no control or forewarning. Some of these situations are certainly what we'd consider tragedies. It's unhealthy to philosophize about lessons or growth opportunities if we're skipping over the feelings associated with painful circumstances or jumping too quickly to the next place. Being human demands that we embrace and experience a full range of emotion and feel whatever we're feeling in each moment. It's often only in this way that we can move on from difficult circumstances. But as we journey into the past and as our present self gains some perspective from past to present, it's empowering to own whatever strengths or lessons unfolded from calamity.

The wakeup call of difficult events often presents powerful teachings. "The Triangle Shirtwaist Factory Fire" that occurred in New York City in March of 1911 killed 146 people. Because of those deaths, not only did the officials of New York City realize that the lack of fire codes in high-rise factories contributed to the high number of casualties, but so did municipal governments throughout the Unites States. Within a relatively short time New York City passed new fire, safety and building codes to prevent such disasters from occurring again. Other cities followed by doing the same. It's impossible to say how many lives were saved nationwide because of the new laws and regulations. It's easy for us, as a society, to look at tragedy we aren't personally involved in and learn from the experience. But this example shows how we can honor, and grow from, what's been lost or suffered.

It's even more difficult to look at personal tragedy engulfing our very existence and learn from that. But it's not uncommon for people to look back and feel gratitude for what's come to them through challenging or even life-threatening circumstances. We may all know someone who's had to fight some form of cancer, so prevalent in modern society. Surviving such a wakeup call can spur folks to enjoy life in ways they never dreamed of before their cancer. No matter the test, each life occurrence carries its own opportunity and demands our full participation. None of us wishes for misfortune, but what we survive and struggle through can ultimately make us stronger, happier and more connected to spirit.

Although not realizing it many people don't live in the present but in the past. You can't be fully engaged with life or dream a better future if your experience is rooted in the past. For the person afraid of dogs, since being bitten there has essentially never been a present, only a past with regard to dogs. Yesterday the person was afraid of dogs. Today they're afraid of dogs. Tomorrow they will be... you get the point. Tomorrow will mirror yesterday, which means today will never come. To live in the present, we have to become conscious of who we are and what we're doing. In recognizing we're responding out of habit to something that occurred long ago, we can decide to change. As all change comes from within, we can suggest a hundred things to help someone, yet they must want to help themselves.

Living in the present, the here and now, helps us engage the living world around us and attune to life as it unfolds. We liken this to taking a full, embodied breath rooted in the here and now. This present breath is inherently woven of a rich tapestry of past experience, a vast and open future, and lots of subtle threading in between giving it beauty, depth and texture. Most importantly, this breath is not stuck in responses or constricting emotional patterns determined by what happened long ago. The woman described in Chapter Two yelled at her Chi Gong teacher but didn't realize that in doing so, she was really yelling at someone from her past. As soon as she woke up to this, she began working on the issue and her healing progressed in leaps and bounds.

After discussing these ideas with your clients, you or they may get a sense that something from their past is holding them back. This will help in determining whether you want to try this exercise, or the one discussed in Chapter Eight, *Preventing Soul Loss*, or both.

# CHAPTER SEVEN

# SHAPESHIFTING, SYMBOLS AND
# SHAMANIC REIKI GUIDES

Though not intending to create controversy, we recognize that some of what we've written could fuel a lively debate within Reiki and/or shamanic healing communities. This might be particularly true between those in the Reiki community who have a background in and accept shamanic approaches, and the more traditional Reiki practitioners who don't. But perhaps we'd find just as rich discussions between shamanic practitioners with more systematized training and those without. Airing differing opinions is healthy and should only be encouraged, and when we come to such deliberations with open hearts and minds, our differences can unite instead of separate us.

We do believe that both shamanism and Reiki are living, ever-changing entities, propelled from compassion to suit to the needs and times of the people of those times, and of all sentient life. And although overly rigid systems tend not to last, we respect the important role more conservative approaches serve. Both shamanism and Reiki enjoy increasing acceptance in North America, for instance, due in great part to the influence of traditional and standardized schools. At the same time, history's greatest visionaries notoriously live, think and act out of the box even when those boxes are already out of the mainstream. The most potent shamans we've known in Siberia and other locations have taught us to glean directly from spirit, in whatever way that presents and regardless of how it's perceived or accepted by others.

As an example, in 2001 a group of western shamanic practitioners went on a lengthy trek through diverse regions of Tuva, Siberia, under the auspices of the non-profit organizations Dream Change and the Sacred Earth Network. Their intention was to experience Tuvan culture and its shamanism, as practiced by nine indigenous female shamans. Many shamans and practitioners throughout the world use the drum to connect to spirit. It's often the case that when this approach is taught in the West, the drum is struck in rapid monotone beats and practitioners are instructed that the purpose is to ride the drum beat into the spirit world. Some shamanic groups blatantly discourage any variation to that monotone drum beat. The trekkers were soon to learn a simple but powerful lesson from women whose ancestors first coined the term shaman: how we perform healing and access spirit doesn't depend on what others think or do. It's facilitated by our personal engagement with spirit, our ability to interpret spirit's whisperings and allow the most beneficial energies to act through us.

The group participated in numerous drumming fire rituals throughout the trip, in villages dotting the Siberian steppe to the Mongolian border, in an all-night ceremony on a mountain-top, and a ceremony to stop the rains in order to safely travel out of an isolated, bogged valley. The members had never encountered the kind of drumming done in these ceremonies as it wasn't the steady, rhythmic beat they knew from their drumming circles back home. Instead, in each ceremony, the Tuvan shamans wove a wild cacophony of song, dance and discordant drumming. When the visiting group was invited to drum alone, the rugged, Siberian women laughed at them, the contrast made it easy to see why. The western practitioners followed patterns they had always used, drumming almost in unison. However, each Tuvan accessed spirit uniquely, in communion with the spirits, energies and ancestors they channeled. Their methods had no discernible form, in fact appearing like a hodge-podge of rhythms. Yet each ceremony generated power. Two people who were dangerously ill recovered during the mountain ceremony. Villagers felt their energy renewed, and as those trapped in the bogged valley did ceremony, the clouds parted before their eyes, the rain stopped, and a rainbow magically arched the skies. They safely drove out the next morning.

Form can be powerful, but ultimately it's our relationship with spirit that fuels the forces that heal and transform. Maybe it's not so imperative for all of us to be exactly on the same page in this respect. But it is important to support each person's and culture's contribution to the evolving story of healing ourselves and our planet.

That said, in the past few chapters you've read about how to use powerful and empowering imaginative journeys with those you work with. This chapter will introduce ways you can use these same journey techniques to strengthen your own connection to Reiki and spirit, not only for insight and knowledge but to deepen the trust essential for this work.

Since Chapter One when we first spoke about the journey process, we've illustrated many possible uses and approaches. Journeying isn't difficult, though beginners tend to build their own obstacles to contacting the realm of spirit. As we've said before, going into the spirit reality is nothing more than closing our eyes and daydreaming we're there. But we'll make a simple suggestion now that intensifies our ability to navigate other worlds, *Cultivating an Inner Sanctum*. This is what many shamanic practitioners call the *sacred place*.

## Cultivating an Inner Sanctum or Sacred Place

When you first close your eyes to journey, imagine, and more importantly feel, that you're resting in a place that evokes comfort, safety, healing and sacredness. This can be a place in nature, lying on a sandy beach by the ocean, in a field under a star-lit sky, or on a bed of pine needles in the forest. Or, it could be a room, tent or cabin that's imbued with objects, aromas, colors and textures that evoke these qualities of comfort, safety, healing and sacredness. This place can be familiar to you, an actual location in this reality, or it can arise completely from your imagination. Regardless of whether it's from this reality or the imaginary realms, when you go to your sacred place it will be as real for you as your senses allow it. Always begin by taking several deep, cleansing and refreshing breaths. As you breathe, intend and allow your body to relax so mind and emotions can settle. Now, simply imagine that you are in your sacred place. It's no more difficult than that, and with a little practice you can be there instantly. Ask yourself, what you see, hear, smell and taste. How does your body feel and what do you feel emotionally as you rest in your sacred place? In the beginning, it's helpful to visit your sacred place as often as you can to orient to it, making it easier to go there at any time. You can access the qualities of this place whenever you need them in your life, as well as whenever you intend to journey.

To use your sacred place as a journeying tool simply imagine yourself there at the beginning of any journey. Set your intention for your journey, settle into your sacred place, and then open your mind to what the journey brings. Your sacred place is the perfect container from which to launch into other worlds. It's a safe harbor whose energy will immediately relax, open you, and settle your mind. It's also a familiar place in the alternate reality from which you not only begin, but return to, when the journey's finished. This provides a transitional space that eases your movement between worlds, from this reality, into others, and back again.

As you establish a connection to your sacred place, you may find you're able to journey more deeply. You can incorporate this practice into any journey example we've outlined in this book. And remember, by anchoring the feeling of safety, comfort and the healing you experience in your sacred place into your body, you can evoke its qualities whenever needed, not just before you begin to journey.

The journey process is a wonderful tool for accessing wisdom, energy and power that lies beyond what the mind alone can conceive. Whether we view these experiences as imaginary, archetypal or mythological, the spiritual reality that interfaces the physical is real, accessible, reliable, and as valid as any source we or our clients could seek for insight, healing and guidance.

## Shapeshifting and Merging

A shamanic technique that's often used is called merging, a shapeshifting practice that was introduced in Chapter Five in our work with the elements. We can merge, or *become one with* for a little while, whatever item has qualities we'd like to experience or benefit from. The Quechua peoples shapeshift into the fire of volcanoes to utilize their power for healing. Amazonian warriors and hunters shapeshift into trees in the rainforest for invisibility; Tuvans merge with bird qualities as displayed by their feather headdresses to fly to other worlds and alternate realities; and shamans of many cultures shapeshift into the qualities of animals for flight, agility, to heighten their senses, and for cunning and swiftness. These aspects may assist them in hunting, healing or guiding their communities. They amplify perception in this world and aid in navigating others.

Another of the many reasons shamans use this approach is to understand more about something. Examples in your everyday life could include a tree on your property, a pet or plant at home that isn't doing well, or a room in your home or an office at work that makes you feel uneasy. Merging with these items can be helpful in discovering what the difficulty is. In the example of the person who was bitten by a dog and was still afraid of them, could you conceive of a better way to grapple with a fear of dogs than by becoming that dog and getting its perspective? This tactic would offer a sympathetic angle to myriad problems. And although we can't do that in this reality, in the alternate reality anything is possible.

We've all had the experience of shifting our energy, expression, posture, and even our mind-set and attitudes, when a situation really demanded it. Shapeshifting is innate to all of us. Our ability to embody, to manifest and to experience the energy we focus on, whether merging with an animal, a vision of the self we aspire to be, or even to become invisible, is a powerful tool that everyone can cultivate.

## Merging into, or Shapeshifting with, Reiki Energy

The first shapeshifting journey we'd like to offer is one that strengthens our relationship with, and gives a better understanding of, Reiki. This can also help us understand and experience how inseparable we are from Reiki energy. Even those who've practiced Reiki for many years and are newly considering incorporating shamanic approaches can gain fresh insights this way.

Please reflect back on the first chapter when we described a visualization illustrating how Reiki energy might flow from the universe into a person (a sphere of light in the sky high above you). It will help for you to recall that now. As you begin, set your intention for the journey to merge with the Reiki energy. Then, go to your sacred place, anchor and feel yourself fully there.

When you feel ready, imagine yourself floating up from your sacred place and away from your body in the room, although you shouldn't feel like you've left your body completely, but that your awareness is simply expanding beyond it. As you reach the ceiling, if you're in the house or a building, keep going up through the roof, into the sky, and high into universe. Your intention is to find that sphere of light that you can feel is the source of Reiki. Remember, the sphere of light is our example. Visualize or sense the source of Reiki energy in whatever way that works for you to perceive it. Do what comes naturally throughout this journey, knowing that our suggestions are just templates for experience. Something totally different may happen. If it does, go with that and don't worry that it differs from what we're suggesting.

When you see or sense the Reiki light/energy, hover near it. Feel its warmth, power and loving intention. From safely within your sacred place, take a deep breath and imagine some light from this energy source entering you. A palpable quality of Reiki energy is a harmonious state of unconditional love, the universe offering itself for our higher good. What does it feel like, what are the sensations you feel in allowing this loving, caring and nurturing energy to penetrate you? Take some time with this, then when you're ready and if you're drawn, speak to the ball of light, or whatever form you perceive. When it feels right, ask permission to enter and merge with the Reiki energy source. The answer might not come in your own voice. You may sense, feel or simply intuit without hearing anything. When you do, enter the Reiki energy. Release yourself to meld with and become one with it. Engage all senses, sight, sound, taste, smell, touch, as well as your subtle senses. Don't think about what you're doing, experience it. Be as a child playing in the water for the first time on a hot summer's day. Swim in the energy, bathe in the energy, be the energy.

Then, in the same manner you communicated with the energy source, do so again from within. Whatever you wish to know, whatever insights you wish to gain from this new perspective of being one with Reiki energy, pose these now. Learn from the source how Reiki can deepen your life, your practice and your knowledge. If there are too many questions for one visit, you can always go back. Or you may have no questions at all, yet in merging with the Reiki energy you may experience a knowing or communion that's beyond words, thoughts and agendas. You may gain non-verbal understanding of how to invite this energy to align with you at anytime. Whatever way it happens for you, whatever your experience, stay here for as long as you wish.

Upon leaving, feel gratitude for what you've received and for the experience of merging with the Reiki energy. Return to your sacred place and take your time to transition back into this reality. Wiggle your toes and fingers, stretch, and open your eyes when you're ready, coming fully back into this reality,

**Merging with Healing Symbols**
The following shapeshifting journey is for Reiki practitioners trained in Level Two or above and those who practice non-traditional forms of Reiki, or any other healing modality applying symbols. Each symbol has unique characteristics and is used for a specific purpose such as performing Reiki long-distance healing. But what do we know about the symbols we're using other than how to draw them, their names and suggested purposes, and what was communicated to us about them when we were trained? Through this exercise, we can find out more.

Return to the source of Reiki per the instructions above. Or if you're using a different energy modality, return to your perception of that energy's source. From the perspective of being one with the Reiki light or the energy as you perceive it as explained above, imagine one symbol in your practice taking form and just as you merged with the energy itself, now merge with this symbol. It's beneficial to focus on one symbol per journey so your attention isn't divided and you can really be that symbol.

When in complete harmony with that symbol, feel its energy and subtle qualities being one with you. Again, open all your senses. Seek anything from the symbols you wish to know during the journey. But try not to ask yes or no questions as these only yield yes or no answers, which might not give you all the information you're looking for. Or simply be that symbol while attuning to its intention and essence.

In Reiki, the symbols are infused by the Reiki master teacher into the energy field of the practitioner. The more we invoke and merge with the symbols that have been implanted and activated within us, the more they integrate into our consciousness and energy system. They become one with us. This practice highlights this relationship, making us more aware of it. Shapeshifting into, or merging with, the Reiki symbols can deepen our healing practice because we embody the symbols whose energy we wish to apply, as opposed to viewing them as separate, something we apply only compartmentally. When adept at shapeshifting into or merging with the symbols during the journeying process, working with them in Shamanic Reiki sessions (and in the attunement process, for Shamanic Reiki master teachers) can become more textured. New ways of invoking the symbols may come or we may be guided to apply them in novel ways, visualizing or sensing instead of drawing symbols, even camaying them into our client's body or energy field. When we open to whatever comes, the unfolding can be ecstatic.

**More about Reiki and Other Healing Symbols**

Mikao Usui re-discovered Reiki energy when he found the secrets for channeling the life force for healing in ancient Tibetan Buddhist sutras. Later Usui prayed, fasted and meditated on the holy Mt Kurama in Japan, entering an altered state of consciousness and receiving the key to transmitting this energy. This is akin to the Buddha's experience of enlightenment under the Bodhi tree or the story from the Nordic tradition of Odin, who sat in a tree, entered a trance state, and received the entire Rune system.

These are the stories of those we might view as being on spiritual pedestals, feeling ourselves quite inept to accomplish anything similar. But we can. These scenarios aren't so different from the vision quests of North American indigenous traditions, which many modern people now embark upon. The quester spends days alone in the desert or the mountains fasting and praying, resulting in an altered state of consciousness during which a vision is received from spirit.

We've all experienced expanded states during our ordinary day. Have you ever had an *ah-ha* moment when something finally clicks, when out of the blue you think Aunt Eunice is going to call, the phone rings and it's her; or have a flash or feeling for something deep inside and it happens? These occurrences are very natural and they happen to all of us. We may move in and out of alternate reality accessing wisdom, power and energy without even noticing it. But for Shamanic Reiki practitioners, this process becomes finely attuned because we cultivate it for the benefit of others.

As we immerse in spirit and Reiki energy, we straddle many worlds and expanded states in the course of a session. In doing so, it sometimes happens that practitioners receive their own symbols. Not theirs actually, but symbols that spirit may present to the practitioner to be used for specific areas of healing or to expand consciousness. This can happen unexpectedly during meditation or even in a healing session. Practitioners can even journey to their guides to obtain symbols for particular needs.

If a new symbol comes, don't dismiss it as being just your imagination. Honor the fact that spirit is whispering to you by listening and journeying to the new symbol, using the merging techniques outlined above. If you're a master teacher and a symbol arrives that helps your practice, include it with the standard Reiki symbols in your attunements. However, it's important to distinguish the new from the originally transmitted symbols, giving your students the background of the new symbol. And for first level Reiki practitioners as well as those employing a modality that doesn't use symbols, the above doesn't preclude you. If, while in your practice a symbol pops into your awareness, draw it in this reality so you can remember it, then journey to it as we've suggested. You can shapeshift into and get to know its energy, as well as ask in what way it would like to be used and for what purposes.

In *Essential Reiki*, Diane Stein states that she learned there were possibly 300 Reiki symbols in existence at one time, with 22 in regular use. In traditional Reiki schools there are five symbols that remain. It's impossible to discern if the symbols that practitioners receive are of the original system of healing from Tibetan texts. But Shamanic Reiki practitioners can journey to ask for a symbol that may help them heal a specific issue. They can also journey to, and shapeshift into, symbols which may appear to them spontaneously so they can understand how to use them. When desiring to do so, simply follow the journeying examples cited above.

Again, the practice of Reiki isn't a static modality. Unlike a mountain, tall and powerful, unmoving in its strength and resolve, practicing Reiki is more like flowing with a river – moving, fluid, shifting – with the speed, direction, force and destination consonant to the circumstances. In deepening our understanding of Reiki and other modalities through shamanic methods, the experiences we have are tailor-made for us and our clients, and what's most needed at the time. Repeat the journeys in a year and some of the answers and experiences may be different. That's why we leave the questions of what to ask both the energy source and the symbols up to you, not delineating what your experience will be. Our questions and experiences may not be yours.

**Finding Your Shamanic Reiki Spirit Guide**
At the core of any shamanic practice, regardless of where in the world it's practiced, is the belief that anyone can access the world of spirit to seek help and guidance. Up until now in this chapter, we've accessed the spirit realm of our own accord by establishing our sacred place and by merging with the energy force and symbols. To engage spirit on another very intimate level, we can establish a relationship with a personal Shamanic Reiki healing guide. The formula we suggest next is as ageless as shamanism.

In our brief discussion of the shamanic journey at the beginning of this book, we mentioned that often the first journey people take into the spirit reality is to find a guide. In many cases, that guide takes the shape of an animal, but it could also appear as a person or object. It's important to establish a relationship with our guide (or guides) and to know that finding one isn't difficult. Earlier, we suggested that you imagine rising up into the sky to seek the source of Reiki. Now, instead of imagining going up, after you've anchored within your sacred place, imagine yourself going down. It's easiest just to feel yourself sinking through the floor and into the earth.

Allow yourself to travel down awhile, so your left-brain knows you've left this reality, and imagine yourself coming out into a world that looks exactly like ours. You may find yourself in a forest, in a meadow, by a stream, on a beach, or literally anywhere. What's the difference, you may ask, between this world and ours if they look alike? In our world, people communicate and things appear solid. In the spirit world, everything is alive, mutable, and can communicate with us. Just as you spoke to the Reiki energy, just as you asked your client to speak to the higher self of a person energetically connected to them or to their own higher self, you call out now for your spirit guide. Who or what do you call out to? Whatever you sense, imagine or intuit that's present (rocks, trees, clouds or other), remembering that everything in the spirit reality can communicate with us. Keep in mind that these guides are often just waiting to be discovered and are excited to begin working with you, so they may appear quickly.

Don't have any expectations, but accept whatever guide comes, from a lion, a ball of light, to a mouse or wizened master. All spirit guides wield power and this power isn't linked to size, weight or appearance, as happens in our world. Ask if this is your Shamanic Reiki guide. No words may be spoken. If you perceive the answer is yes then you can begin. But if you sense the answer is no, simply ask it to please take you to your Shamanic Reiki guide. Allow this daydream to evolve a life of its own. Flow with it remembering that you can do, and be, anything you wish. If you feel the urge to follow your guide and it flies off, imagine yourself on its back, or that you're a bird or have a power pack strapped on your back to fly off with it. Or simply feel the innate power to jump into the air and keep going. It doesn't matter and you won't fall.

## Working With Your Shamanic Reiki Guide

Once you've found your guide, open your mind and your senses to it. We all have different orientations so although many people will vividly see their guides in the journey space, some will only sense them. Our guides are identifiable through their energy, so sensing or feeling them is as good as seeing them with your inner vision. You might consider asking some questions of your guide and below are only examples: Why are you my guide? What do I need to know in order to deepen my Shamanic Reiki practice? How can you help with my practice? What's the most important thing you can communicate to me about working with you in healing sessions?

These are just a few suggestions. Your own questions are the important ones. There are very few basic rules in shamanism, but one of them is having intention and just as Reiki is fueled by our intention, so is the shamanic journey. If you find your mind starting to wander, which is what minds invariably do, just come back to your intention to travel to the spirit world to find a Shamanic Reiki guide.

The second task of this journey, or you may save it for a subsequent journey if it feels like too much for this time, is to shapeshift into the energy of your guide. To do this, simply invite its energy to merge with you as you merged with the Reiki energy. We aren't separate from the energy of our guides, they're archetypal forces that we can access and draw upon. Merging with our guides is a practice we can then evoke during Shamanic Reiki healing sessions. Simply feel your guide as one with you, feel and sense its energy and qualities. Or imagine or feel your guide as vividly as you can directly in front of you. Take a few imaginary steps toward your guide and feel yourself walk into him/her/it, whatever its form. Feel its qualities and energy. Then step back out and feel the difference.

To work with your guides in your practice with clients, follow their input if they've communicated something specific to you. If not, or additionally, you can try shapeshifting into your guide during a session and invite the guide's energy to work through you for the benefit of your client. You can do this at the very beginning of a session, and then re-evoke and strengthen this intention when starting the hands-on work. Really feel your guide's energy, allowing it to work and intuit through you as you allow the Reiki energy to flow.

Shamanic Reiki guides can sometimes appear differently than usual shamanic guides, so be open to what form yours takes. Also know that guides can shapeshift into other forms at any time. Your guide may direct work through you, with flowers, drums, rattles and other items that were noted in Chapter Four. You'll gain the best understanding of how to work with your guide through your experience and relationship with it.

**Many Guides and Many Ways**

Spirit guides can come and go, so don't be surprised if another shows up or if a favored one leaves. You can have many at one time or work with only one. It depends on spirit, and if you hope to apply any linear logic to spirit's ways, good luck – you'll only become frustrated. And again, curb the tendency to analyze whatever information you may cull from a journey while in the journey state. Just experience it and remember as much as you can. Then write the journey down as soon as possible because they have the evaporative quality of nighttime dreams, and can be hard to remember. Once fully back in this reality, you can analyze all you wish. But you'll find accessing the messages a richer experience when your heart and body are as engaged as your mind.

Shamanic Reiki practitioners call on their guides during a session, when speaking with clients, when intuiting how to help clients and when attuning or teaching Shamanic Reiki to others. If we have many guides, we can ask in which areas they'll be most helpful, or discern this by feeling it. Our guides can become powerful allies when we let them.

**Deepening the Practice**

We earlier discussed the Tuvan shamans who approached spirit differently than each other and than their western guests, the way other shamans or shamanic practitioners drummed had no relevance for them. These shamans gleaned through experience, success and trust, what to do and how to go about it. Just as each of these shamans' methods of calling upon spirit differed from their colleagues, we can develop our own intimate walk with the healing modality we practice. This is what empowers our work beyond the techniques we've been taught.

After you've tried and experienced some of the exercises in this chapter, you may want to include them in your practice. You can also selectively pass any of them on to your Shamanic Reiki clients. We can all benefit from establishing an inner sanctum or sacred place. There's a place in all of our lives for shapeshifting or merging, and we can empower those who come to us for Shamanic Reiki by helping them discover their own Shamanic Reiki guides. The only thing to discern is which approach to use, when, and with which client. As mentioned in previous chapters, journeys can be difficult. Calling upon, or merging with, our guides can help us decide whether a particular exercise will be beneficial to a person. And by now it should be obvious that altering any journey suggested (in this or any other chapter) is not only completely fitting, but encouraged. In this way we can better meet the unique needs and circumstances of our clients.

# CHAPTER EIGHT

# TIME TRAVELING TO PREVENT
# SOUL LOSS

For simplicity's sake, removing from its definition any religious connotations, we'll define the word soul as: the vital living essence of who we are now, have been in the past, or who we could be in the future. Using this framework, we can consider that the word soul implies our core self or essential qualities. This essential self is inseparable from, yet also spans beyond, our body, circumstances, personality, and even our mortality. Because the soul is one with present time and space, yet also radiates beyond this awareness, the soul has access to boundless wisdom. Our soul, as our spiritual core, links us to all times and places and to a larger, universal and intelligent source.

Some find it helpful to concretize this idea that the soul is an individuated consciousness connected to a superior origin, like a ray of sunlight separate from, though indivisible from its source. Yet unlike the sun (origin/source) which is fixed in space, this light-ray (soul) can travel to the earth and infuse itself into the physical life on this planet. Since ancient times, people have accepted the notion that each of us has a soul, the sinew that binds the fabric of our human potential, enabling us to express ourselves uniquely. In short, the soul is a person's essential or core aspect of being. But how do we experience the soul and recognize its influence in our daily lives?

We may know the soul as that which infuses us with life and inspires us to achieve beyond self-serving interests, to pause and watch a sunset, to fulfill important obligations even when we're exhausted, to dance or to paint a picture, to be patient and compassionate with others, to think and act in consonance with who we really are despite others expectations, or to simply leave the house and take a walk. But if we don't experience it this way, it's possible that our soul is incomplete.

## Concept

On an absolute level our soul is always intact, whole and complete, just as we are ultimately, and always, inseparable from spirit and Reiki energy. But from a shamanic point of view we can feel separated from, and need to reconnect with, facets of our soul, just as we can feel separated from, and need to reconnect with, spirit and Reiki energy. Shamans the world over believe that shocking or painful events can trigger partial soul flights from the body, leaving a traumatized person with a fragmented or incomplete soul. This splintering of the soul not only blocks us from expressing our higher aspects, the part of us aspiring to act in harmony with the universe, but may also instigate behavior in direct conflict with our true or deeper self.

Sandra Ingerman, a western shamanic teacher generally accepted as one of the leading practitioners in the field of soul retrieval, believes that when we experience an event that we consider to be traumatic, part of our soul may flee. This happens as a survival mechanism, protecting the individual from experiencing the full force of the painful circumstance.

We've used the image of a ray of sunlight for the soul. Let's explore another impression to understand how, on a relative level, a soul can be incomplete.

Imagine the soul as a 500-piece jigsaw puzzle. When viewing the intact puzzle, we have a complete soul picture of one person. Our soul would consist of the 500 varying sized and shaped pieces comprising one puzzle, each piece representing a facet of the soul's character. To envisage an incomplete soul, conceive the puzzle pieces being disassembled, out of place, or that several pieces are out of view altogether. Although all the soul qualities are there, the pieces aren't put together correctly. Looking at such a puzzle, we couldn't discern the whole picture so we wouldn't be able to perceive this person's essence. And they wouldn't be able to express the totality of who they are. In cases of soul loss, people can appear vacant, emotionally repressed, chronically depressed, or even extremely imbalanced. All can reflect disassociated soul parts, or a jumbled or incomplete soul puzzle picture, according to our analogy.

The trauma that causes the soul to fragment is not always apparent. If a person is physically attacked, in a car accident, returning from war, or experiences the loss of a parent, child or loved one, the trauma is obvious. In other, subtler instances, the trauma may not seem like a major life event to anyone but the person who disassociates from part of their vital essence. For instance, children raised in the same environment may interpret and experience family events very differently. Trauma needs to be defined in personal terms as an incident appearing innocuous and carrying no emotional charge for one person, may cause another's soul piece to drop away. With that essential part of them missing, that person's engagement with life will somehow be restricted.

Imagine a seven-year-old child who loves to dance but has been told not to dance in the living room. One day the child spontaneously dances around the sofa to a well-loved song on the radio. In doing so she knocks into a coffee table, causing her mother's favorite vase to fall and break. The mother screams violently at the child, sending her off to her room. In a few moments, the mother goes to her daughter's room, hugs her, kisses her tears away, and tells her she still loves her. Everything appears fine for the time being. However, the child doesn't dance in the house anymore, and her demeanor becomes more controlled. Being yelled at in the midst of such a joyous moment caused some of the child's vibrancy to leave her. The puzzle piece that was jarred out of place was an aspect of the child's spontaneity, and that missing aspect may affect the child's future behavior, even into adulthood. She'll continue to be impacted until she reunites with that fragmented piece of her soul puzzle.

Most shamans perceive soul fragmenting as occurring many times throughout our lives. Although the little girl mentioned above lost or dislodged a part of her soul, our analogy shows that she still has 499 puzzle pieces in place. Yet each piece is susceptible to being dislodged, although depending on the person and circumstance, some of us are more vulnerable to soul splintering than others. When our essence self does suffer fragmentation, we live with dis-harmony and dis-ease, regardless of the state of our physical health. This is why the concept of repairing soul loss is so important.

Finding and returning a disassociated piece of a soul puzzle to its owner is called *soul retrieval*. It's important to note that there are as many ways of performing soul retrievals as there are perspectives about what constitutes a soul. Siberian and Mongolian shamans believe humans have three distinct souls, all of which can be jolted from the body during trauma. In their retrievals, Andean Quechua peoples we know interweave soul call-backs as they apply plants, stones and sacred items during healings. Some, invoking the energy of sacred volcanoes by engulfing their naked clients in balls of fire, say the soul aspects automatically fly back to the person in the process.

This section wouldn't be complete without acknowledging other approaches, body-mind and energetic, which also heal on the soul level, restoring lost essential qualities. Accessing energy, wisdom and power from other worlds to benefit our own world isn't restricted to those of indigenous heritage. As John Perkins points out, "We are all descendant from shamanic indigenous peoples anyway." This is said in an even simpler way by Brazilian Amazonian elder, Ipupiara Makunaiman, "We are all shamans!"

Although rarely identified as such by their culture, there's an abundance of contemporary teachers and healers we could rightly call shamans. Many are visionaries gleaning methods directly from spirit, intuition, the muses, the collective unconscious or whatever they may call it. And many, such as Body-Centered Tranformation, Continuum, Somato Respiratory Integration, EMDR (Eye Movement Desensitization Reprocessing) and Hypnotherapy, to name just a few, use and evoke strikingly shamanic processes to restore vital, essential connections. Some are specifically successful in helping trauma victims and those suffering Post Traumatic Stress Disorder, afflictions typically associated with soul loss.

Along the same vein, Reiki energy and attunements also reunite us with vital essential parts of our soul. This, in part, is why Reiki works so well with shamanism as it does with the above modalities. The Reiki master attunement and symbol, in particular, cleanses and aligns us on the soul level. Methods, origin and appearance may differ, but many ancient as well as modern systems can assist in retrieving vital, lost soul energies.

That said, for the sake of our discussion, we'll focus here on the soul retrieval technique most familiar to the modern shamanic practitioner, that of journeying into the spirit world on someone's behalf to find and return that disassociated piece. Experienced teachers of this form of soul retrieval will assert that only those with specified training should perform them. The reasons are justified:

1) It is necessary to have a strong relationship to the helping spirits guiding us in and out of the worlds these lost soul parts inhabit.
2) It takes a skillful practitioner to interact with the soul piece and determine the appropriateness and timing of calling it back.

If intrigued by the concept, there's no better resource than Sandra Ingerman's books, *Soul Retrieval, Mending The Fragmented Self* and *Welcome Home, Life After Healing Following Your Soul's Journey Home.*

Even though only experienced shamanic practitioners should attempt soul retrievals we emphasize that there are still many things a Shamanic Reiki practitioner can do to help a client with soul loss.

**Preventing Soul Loss**

We aren't suggesting that Shamanic Reiki practitioners perform soul retrievals requiring advanced expertise, in fact, we advise against it. But, in speaking with clients we may discover a specific past event that's triggered a flight response and the person has suffered soul loss. When identified, it's possible to assist our clients in time-traveling to that specific occurrence to prevent the loss from happening in the first place.

The difference between soul retrieval and preventing soul loss is that retrievals restore the soul or essence piece back to the person after a lengthy stay in another world. Vital pieces have fled to take safe harbor in other realms and don't return when the danger's passed. Soul loss prevention immediately returns the energy, or convinces it not to leave the moment it's impelled to do so. In the spiritual reality, time isn't a relative phenomenon. As past, present and future occur simultaneously, we can access the exact moment of fragmentation, to replace or reorient the soul or puzzle piece almost immediately after, or just as it leaves.

Detecting soul loss in a person comes with experience. But one general guideline is that we look for significant and long-term changes in personality and/or health after a traumatic event. This can be obvious and observable to those close to the person such as with a loved one having difficulty getting over a spouse's death. Or it may be more obscure, as in the case of an outwardly successful, highly organized woman who danced freely as a child but now rarely acts spontaneously.

It's helpful to trust our Shamanic Reiki guides, use our instincts, and to observe our client's energy, emotional tone and body language, all of which can signal soul splintering. Likely, when souls take flight under duress, the body is also engaged in a flight response, of the classic physiological fight or flight syndrome. As a fragmented soul will reveal its wounding we just need to read the signs. Notice the quality of your client's breathing, especially whether it's shallow, choppy or cut off at the chest. How do they move and hold themselves, do they appear constricted or awkward? Does your client speak minimally and avoid eye contact or are they incessant talkers? Is there a distracted quality, a sense of not being fully present? Can you feel the person's emotional patina or is there a sense that nobody's home? Or do they talk about feeling that something is missing? Being out of touch with our deeper aspects means we can't fully participate with life, as we have to be fully in our bodies to do this. When there is soul loss, a part of our spirit hovers outside of us so it's nearly impossible to fully inhabit our bodies and emotions.

When the possibility of soul loss strikes a cord with someone who's actively engaged in their own healing, practitioner and client can work together to restore essential energies. And although this can be one of the most empowering exercises someone can undertake, it can be challenging. Journeying back in time to sorrowful circumstances isn't easy, but allows us to see from a different perspective. It helps us understand how events can cause part of our vitality to diminish, affecting and changing us in ways we're likely not happy with now. Although we can't do anything about what's already happened, we can attempt to regain a sense of the person we were before the incident, or of the person whom we now most wish to be.

Remember that soul loss occurs when a person experiences an event that's perceived as life changing. If the circumstances are right, losing a lucky charm your grandmother gave you before she died could be a life-changing event. But, usually, there's a behavioral or health alteration after the soul loss, and as time passes, the person often accepts these shifts as something they can't change. An example would be the woman who danced as a child and longs to be more impulsive but now believes her constricted personality is simply who she is.

It's important to speak with your clients before engaging in any shamanic work, as in reconfiguring the energy connected to past events or with preventing soul loss. The event you're focusing on must be clearly targeted and your client must understand the process and agree that it's a helpful one to pursue. You don't have to be a therapist to engage in these discussions, though part of this work pushes the envelope of Shamanic Reiki counselor, especially as its effects can be immediate and dramatic. Because of this it's wise to make sure your client has a healthy network of friends and family to call upon for extra support. If they haven't already secured a therapist beyond the work they're doing with you, they should also leave your healing space with a list of local referrals. It's important to make sure clients are ready for, and supported in, the shifts that may occur. Creating conscious environment is also essential to this support, and we urge you to read Chapter Ten, *Creating a Sacred Container for Your Work*, before trying the practices below.

The Shamanic Reiki practitioner's critical ingredients for assisting clients to time-travel to the past to prevent soul loss are to have clear intentions, to be caring individuals, and to have the spiritual health of their clients as their primary concern. Since you'll be conducting this session as a Shamanic Reiki practitioner, you should know that every-thing that occurs within the session will be guided by the intelligence of Reiki energy. Therefore, trust yourself, trust spirit, and trust the universal life force. Level Two Reiki practitioners and higher can use the Reiki symbols.

**Time Traveling to Prevent Soul Loss**

Before the hands-on part of the Shamanic Reiki session, we speak with our client about traveling back in time to prevent soul loss. We ask the person to imagine traveling back in time to the place where the targeted event happened. The object will be for them to be a third party watching the event from above. Our clients must witness the event itself, but from a detached perspective, watching their past self as circumstances un-fold. The person must be clear about the intention for the journey before it begins: "I wish to see the part of my soul – or vital energy – just as it leaves my body. When this happens, I wish to prevent this part of my essence from leaving me."

In terms of what the soul part or essence energy will look like there's no answer that fits everyone as we're all unique. As examples: it could be a soft flowing energy shape exiting from the heart, or the adult going back to view her child-self dancing and being yelled at might see a luminous, yet defined ballerina shape leaving her body. Our clients need initially only to view their past self as the event occurs. They can assume that whatever they see, sense or intuit leaving their body is their soul or essence aspect. How they perceive this or what it looks like isn't as important as what they do when they see it.

The more difficult (traumatic) the event, the harder it may be to stop the soul part from leaving. We stress that they're not to re-live the incident emotionally, but to witness it from a detached perspective, as if watching a movie starring a past self. Remind your client in the beginning that they can stop the experience at any time, they are in control. When able to see the soul's aspect leave their body, the task is simply to persuade it not to go and to immediately return it to their body. Instead of having a soul retrieval performed in the present by a shamanic practitioner, our clients prevent the soul loss from occurring in the first place. Preventing one's own essential qualities from leaving can be challenging, but is extremely empowering.

Clients accomplish this in any way that comes to them during their imaginative journey. The first thing to consider is holding the soul part and hanging onto it if the part continues to move away. They can shout to it, whisper to it, beg it, coax, and bargain with it, whatever seems most natural given the circumstances. It's helpful to discuss this process with clients before their journey, so they have a sense of how they can convince the soul part to stay.

When we have the soul part's attention, communication should happen quickly to give it the most information in the shortest time. That way, we can keep the soul piece from moving further away. The person begins by telling the essence part who they are and that they've arrived from the future to heal this exact moment. The person shares details of what's transpired since the event and why it's so important for the soul part to stay in (return to) the body. The woman who broke the vase, for example, tells the soul aspect what she's missed out on because her spontaneity was curtailed. She can detail the many positive and happy things that will become possible after the event, despite the trauma. The client should stress that regardless of the severity of the event he or she will overcome it and move on. The essence piece needs to know that life continues after the incident.

Again, in this conversation, clients maintain focus on their past self during the event, and as soon as part of their vital essence leaves, they ignore whatever else is happening to their past self and attend only to the soul piece. They are not to be concerned with the impact of the event itself. The point of this journey is solely to get the soul part or vital energy to return to their body. Once that happens, the client can end the journey and come back to ordinary reality.

### Session Notes for Preventing Soul Loss
During the session, the client does most of the work. We open the hands-on part of our Shamanic Reiki session the way we always do. Then when the person appears totally relaxed we'll whisper for them to go to their sacred place as outlined in the previous chapter. From there, they can begin the journey of traveling to the past. Again we suggest keeping Shamanic Reiki hands in one place. A good region to rest the hands is on the forehead or with the palms meeting at the crown and hands cupped on either side of the temples. Be aware that any movements the body makes,

such as shaking or twitching, often signal energetic releases associated with the trauma. This is a good sign. You can keep your hands where they are, simply witnessing the release, or move them gently to what areas draw you.

Depending on the person you're working with, there may be dialoguing during the journey state. A soft and steady voice is grounding and it's important to not get caught up in associations or projections regarding your client's target. In other words, don't get emotionally involved with what they're focusing on. Keep in mind the several ways clients can convince soul parts to return if they ask for help during their journey. Release expectation in process and outcome, letting your guides and Reiki work through you. Remain a steady, supportive force whose presence your client can count on and keep coming back to.

If you're a Level Two practitioner or above, you can send Reiki to the past circumstance and apply the mental/emotional symbols as you do so. Reiki master teachers and practitioners can apply the master symbol, effective in soul-level integrating. If at Level One, simply channel Reiki to what areas draw you. The universal life force envelopes your client in love, healing and protection. Reiki provides a sacred container from which your client can safely revisit an event they may likely have spent a lot of time trying to forget.

It's best to have a prearranged signal to indicate when the journey's complete, raising and lowering a hand, for example, or having the client simply say "Done." You can complete the hands-on part of the session at this time, but intuit the appropriateness of asking your client to turn over to work on their back. Reiki helps your client assimilate the soul part within the body and integrate the experience of traveling to a different time frame. Additionally, it offers the powerful tool of touch, non-verbally communicating support as clients incorporate emotional and energetic aspects of their journey.

All sessions should have enough time built-in for people to reorient before leaving your healing space and to share what feels appropriate. In this case, it's imperative to do so. Trust your instincts in dialoguing with your client. It can be helpful for clients to express how they felt during the journey, and also upon returning to this reality. Do they feel any different now that their soul part or vital energy has returned? If so, what are some of these feelings? If they don't feel immediately different remind them that change can unravel slowly.

If your healing space is near a forest or park, it's ideal for people to go outside after a preventing soul loss journey, asking nature to help them stabilize and complete whatever needs completing. There are some good discussions about this in Chapter Five, and here's another example below:

*Simply take a leisurely walk or wander awhile until drawn to a healthy tree. Sitting on the earth with your back to the tree, breathe slowly and deeply, clearly imagining – or sensing/feeling – the roots of the tree extending deeply into the earth. Then, continuing to breathe, also feel the space all around the tree, and with your awareness, travel up through the trunk and branches, extending out to the sky and heavens above you. Have the intention for the tree to help you anchor your essence qualities firmly into you. Breathe in this awareness, as well as replenishing energy from the earth and heavens through the vehicle of the tree. Also at this time, invite the tree to remove anything outdated that wants to leave you – breathing circumstances, feelings, habits, energies, physical conditions, out into the tree. The tree immediately absorbs then transmutes these into positive energy. Then on each in-breath that follows, feel your body, mind and emotions infused with vibrant energy, healing and power. Connect in these ways until you feel awake and grounded. Before leaving, express your gratitude to the tree for its assistance by leaving a small piece of bread or some loose tobacco.*

This practice is integrating, stabilizing and ideally continued at home, especially as people can feel vulnerable following these sessions. Remind clients that they can journey anytime to this same tree, or make a similar connection with a tree on their own land, or in a park or forest near them. Be sure people don't drive until fully grounded and be available for extra session or phone times if needed. Encourage conscious and gentle attention upon returning home.

This exercise of *Preventing Soul Loss* can be challenging. But Shamanic Reiki practitioners find that changing past energy and preventing soul loss are powerful shamanic tools. Follow your guidance in relationship to the unique person you're working with. Exactly how things are done, the conversations you have with your client, the guidance you offer during sessions – evolve with experience and change with circumstance. Adapting any of the above details is justified when the motivation for doing so is your client's well-being.

### Integrating the Soul Part or Vital Energy

If your client returns from the journey with renewed personal power, an expanded view of their lives, and confident that they can express the energy or attribute of their missing soul piece, the integration of that vital part was spontaneous. The puzzle piece has returned to its proper place, orientating itself back into the puzzle. This is ideal. But, of course, it doesn't always work that way. What if they don't feel anything different at all? If this is the case, it's important that the client returns for a session to integrate the energy or soul part. Soul integration is a necessary component and can't be overlooked. There are many ways of doing this, yet we're going to suggest one, a simple technique clients can do at home or with you. To comprehend the process more fully, it can be helpful to read how Sandra Ingerman presents it in the books mentioned above.

Before clients leave your healing space, explain that preventing a soul part or vital aspect of themselves from leaving is just the first step in the healing process. Clients must now integrate that part with the rest of their vital living essence. On an absolute level, the spiritual plane, the soul part or vital energy was never really lost. But despite this, if the integration isn't complete, the fact that this part has been missing all these years will feel pronounced.

Again, let's use the example of the little girl who broke the vase at age seven. Say that now, at age 30, she journeys back through time to prevent that loss. The missing part of her spontaneity comes back, or more correctly, it's never left her in the first place. If the integration is spontaneous, this woman will feel her new self as perfectly natural, her constricted past personality dream-like and no longer characterizing her. If the integration isn't complete, the countless times she's constricted herself in the past 23 years will still feel very real. In this case, accepting her new self may seem difficult. To remedy this, she must integrate with the restored piece of her essence. The journey presented below offers a simple way to do this:

If the journey's done in the next session, begin as with any Shamanic Reiki session. When you sense the person is ready, invite them to their sacred place, and to let you know when they're fully there, utilizing all their senses. Now, from that protected, safe and healing place, ask the person to call upon the form the soul part took in their last journey. Call that part into their sacred place. Ask them to see, feel, or imagine this part appearing. When it arrives, the two must dialogue. There's no trauma occurring now. In the peaceful atmosphere of their sacred place, your client can thank this part of their vitality for coming back, and express everything to it that compels them. They can say anything they wish. Yet in closing, the intention motivating this journey must be honored by asking this soul piece, "What can I do to support you now, how can I really make you part of my living essence?" In the girl's case she may explain: "I do know that you've been with me since the vase broke, but in reviewing and feeling my life since that time, I see and still feel the impact of how you've been missing for me. What can I do to become fully one with you again?" Please note that these are our questions and perhaps not exactly the ones you will be drawn to suggest.

When the person signals that the journey is done, complete the rest of the session, then discuss what the soul part said. Per the above example, it may be as simple as dancing around the living room or having a hot fudge sundae for dinner that night. Remember, the adult woman must embrace the seven-year-old part of herself and really feel as if that part has completely merged with the adult personality. Dancing in the living room or eating that ice cream may be all that's needed. But if a second or third journey is needed, she can do them at home alone.

People usually return from *Preventing Soul Loss* journeys with positive results. Occasionally they can't persuade the part to return. You can then repeat the journey on another day. Or, you can ask your client to do the following journey that has a completely different intent, to stop the soul part or vital energy from leaving by enticing it to take safe harbor in your sacred place.

In this journey, the person again tells the soul piece everything outlined in the first journey, but instead of asking it not to leave or to return to the body, they take a different tactic. They acknowledge to this vital aspect of themselves how traumatic the event was, and what a wise thing it is to flee, hide and restore right now. Then they describe their sacred place and ask, "Wouldn't this be a soothing, nurturing and healing place to rest for the time being?" If the description is alluring enough, the soul part or essential piece of them will go there. Once it does, they can thank it, and invite it to remain there as they leave. Later, they can return – either in the same session or in a subsequent one. They converse with this part of them in the serene enclosure of their sacred place, employing the same conversation of asking the soul part to return. The necessity for speed isn't present now as the conversation is carried out in the protective environment of the sacred place. This time, the part should say yes and the intention of the journey is completed. Instead of going back to the time of the event, the part is simply asked to merge with the person and return to their life essence. If this is the journey your client takes before merging with the soul part, add the integrating journey that was just described.

**Bringing it Home**

Preventing soul loss isn't easy or simple, and doesn't always translate into instant harmony. The process can require several journeys and several sessions before clients feel a soul part has fully integrated with their current self. But, as noted before, this may be one of the most empowering journeys you facilitate for clients. Once soul healing commences, unexplainable un-ease can dissolve and healing can ensue for what's gone underground or festered since a shocking incident.

If the person is a shamanic practitioner or energetically adept we'll give them the option of doing both journeys, *Removing Deleterious Cords* and *Preventing Soul Loss*, at the same time. First, they'll view the event with the intent to remove energetic cords. Then they'll focus on the same event while watching for a soul part to leave. Events traumatic enough to necessitate cord removal usually also induce soul loss, so both journeys are typically warranted, either at the same time or in separate sessions.

As a Shamanic Reiki practitioner, when you sense there's an event from a client's past that requires soul loss prevention, don't be afraid to suggest this journey. But remember that gentle, alert attention is required. Support from the Reiki energy, a wakeful environment, and your Shamanic Reiki guides, allows clients to prevent soul loss without reliving the experience of the trauma. Again, clients are only to view the scene from a detached perspective, as if watching a movie of a past self. And yet, don't take this journey lightly as it can bring to consciousness events that have long been suppressed.

There are challenges to this journey, yet they're usually well worth the gain. Greater closure can come for painful events, and in merging with soul energies, vitality is restored and a deep sense of wholeness experienced. In helping others retrieve essential qualities, you facilitate their highest expression. In doing so, you help to transform our world.

# CHAPTER NINE

# SHAMANIC REIKI AND PAST LIVES

Hopefully, you're comfortable at this stage of reading with the marvel called shamanism and see how easily it integrates with Reiki healing. If you've accepted Shamanic Reiki's validity, you've likely experienced firsthand some of the approaches outlined, or adaptations gleaned from what you've read. With any luck your healing basket is by now a cornucopia of creative, flexible and powerful methods you can draw upon to benefit others. In this chapter, we'll offer a concept more broadly applied than shamanism, one that spans philosophies and cultures around the world. If at first this idea feels too far out for you, please consider just tacking it onto the edge of your healing basket for the time being. Hold final judgment until after you've tried these techniques. We trust that when you're ready you'll deem them worthy of their proper place in your basket.

## Concept

As in exploring the concept of the soul in the previous chapter, the following is offered without religious implication beyond its general link to spirituality: when people die, a part of their being, their essence, their uniqueness continues, and can be reborn as another human life on the earth. This infers that each of us may have lived other lives, past lives, occurring before our present day existence. In our own passing we're also able to convey to our next creation part of who we have been in this lifetime. Additionally, this implies that if an important issue wasn't completed in one lifetime, and still remains unresolved at the time of death, it's possible to resolve the issue(s) the next time around. It's only fair to say that these unresolved issues can be persistent about wanting to be settled. Most shamanic practitioners would agree that a lesson we need to learn will present itself over and over until we get it. If we pass on before getting it, this doesn't mean the lesson ends. It'll play out through other lifetimes until we confront it and initiate new ways of being.

This notion is older than any of today's organized religions and doesn't espouse conventional religious beliefs of an afterlife. There's no definitive answer or logic for how we progress through lifetimes. There are many paths, opinions and philosophies delineating the parameters, including how to secure a better position in the next life and how to remove oneself from the cycle of returning altogether. It would take a separate book to do any of these orientations justice, which isn't our aim. As the thrust of this text is to cultivate a Shamanic Reiki practice, we'll take a practical approach to past lives – to help people become more present and fulfilled in this life.

Some might say that a definition of why *we are who we are*, our human personality, could be the sum total of our heredity, environment and personal experiences. A simple extension to that definition, including the idea of past lives, would read: we are who we are because of the sum total of heredity, environment and personal experiences, as well as those experiences carried into this reality from lives in other times and places. Let's explore how this applies to Shamanic Reiki and how we can discover what past life circumstances are linked to current health, behavioral or relationship patterns for our clients.

Earlier in the text we cited a person who was still afraid of dogs, decades after being bitten by one. What if this fear existed for someone who'd never had a bad experience with a dog? Or imagine a woman who's terrified to stand up to her controlling husband, or a brilliant person who shies away from achievement. Or consider a man with an aversion to medical professionals without any previous medical trauma, or a person perpetuating unhealthy relationships that leave them feeling abandoned. Examples like these sound easy to invent, but we didn't have to invent them to emphasize why knowing about past lives can be important. When do we, as Shamanic Reiki practitioners, look at the possibility of a past life influence? When a person complains about a troubling symptom or issue, or feels held back in ways that haven't shifted after several sessions, and neither the client nor we understand its origin or persistence.

What would we hope to gain from looking into a past life connection relating to a current issue? Let's first explore some answers to the dilemmas above. Those relevant to your own clients will reveal themselves as you explore these techniques on your own.

What if the person never bitten by a dog was attacked and killed by wolves in another lifetime in Alaska? What if the woman with the controlling husband was incarcerated by a man in a previous lifetime, and what if the brilliant under-achiever deserted a past life family to pursue his dreams, at the cost of being rejected by his community? Imagine that the person averse to medical professionals was a late 19th century physician abandoning his profession after making a mistake that killed a young patient, or that the person who feels abandoned was a child living during the Black Plague, forsaken to starve to death after his parents died.

Each of the above problems presented in this life comes with a purportedly real correlate from another lifetime. If this appears hard to believe, please keep reading, as there's plenty of time to decide what feels right and what doesn't.

Remember that linear time does not exist in the shamanic sense – the past, present and future can all blend and become indistinguishable. Therefore, healing a wound that was caused a hundred or a thousand years ago will have the same effect as healing a wound that was caused yesterday. Recall the reference in Chapter Three about intrusions imbedded from wounds inflicted in the far distant past, as this implies that some of these could be past-life wounds. And regarding Chapter Eight's focus on preventing soul loss, it's helpful to recognize that separation from a person's vital essence may not be limited to the soul part fleeing in this lifetime, but can carry forward from past lives into this one.

Wounds and disassociations from trauma not resolved in a person's past life can be held in present day body, emotion and psyche, as well as in a person's energetic and cellular memory. This is why a child may be born with some of its soul pieces already jarred from the puzzle. As we unconsciously perpetuate wounded patterns from moment to moment, it's important to point out that ultimately we aren't just victims. Once we see how we empower our own attitudes and actions, we have the ability to change wounded patterns on the spot. But acknowledging our power to shift dis-ease is often difficult, let alone being able to do anything about it. This is part of why exploring past lives for healing purposes can benefit us. Accessing other times and places makes our choices conscious and opens a path to shifting the energy. And beyond fixing problems and shifting issues, it can also bring insight to our spiritual journey. We can gain a deeper understanding of why we're here, draw upon the gifts and wisdom of other times, and expand our sense of who we are beyond this present life span.

There's mounting evidence for reincarnation and you'll find remarkable cases of children who remember past lives in Tom Shroder's book, *Old Souls*. But in actuality, we don't even have to believe in past lives for the below exercises to work and for healing to happen. If you, or your clients, just can't buy the concept, here's how to approach these methods regardless of philosophical orientation: framed in the simplest way, what holds us back or limits us is a living template of energy impacting us in our present lives. Regardless of where this template originates from, or when, this energy reveals its patterns via stories and pictures. For our purposes here, these pictures and scenarios are what people refer to as past lives. That the story is real or not doesn't matter for healing to happen, it's the energetic pattern the scenario represents that's the important thing. What initially matters is only that we access the story and begin to engage the energy associated with it. That can be accomplished through shamanic journeying.

## Accessing Past Lives

Suppose we have a client who can't break an unhealthy life pattern or who exhibits dis-ease that's stubborn to shift and whose root cause eludes us. The source may be hidden within a past life dynamic, or per our discussion above, an energetic blueprint we haven't yet been able to access or impact. What we'll offer is a shamanic journey to see what appears, to get information and engage the energy. Remember that people journey into the shamanic realms to acquire wisdom, energy and power. Whether they accept the validity of their experience and what they do with it will be up to them.

Offered below are three examples of shamanic journeys that can be facilitated for clients during Shamanic Reiki sessions. As with everything outlined before, once you've read these suggested journeys, please alter, change or invent your own as long as the goal, having clients access past lives or the energetic template (presenting in pictures or stories) impacting their current dilemma, is reached. Extended session times work very well for past-life work, as they do for preventing soul loss and shifting past events. It's important to have sufficient time for the journey itself as well as to prepare and do the follow-up discussion and integration. As this journey can be difficult, clients often need extra time to get grounded before leaving our healing space to return to mundane worldly activities.

For each of these journeys, let clients know that you'll be facilitating a past life viewing for them, but that as you do so, if something happens that's different than what you're saying, or at a faster rate than what you describe, they should feel perfectly comfortable in going with their experience. You can: 1) explain the entire journey before the client begins, 2) whisper one section of the journey at a time, and move on to the next section when the person indicates they've completed what you've just suggested by raising a hand or forearm.

Remember that each of the journeys below is designed with the intention for people to see, sense or intuit what appears within the journey space, to retrieve information in whatever way occurs for them, and to connect with the energetic template that's impacting them from a past life. You'll find discussion on how these experiences, and the information gleaned from them, can be used after the journeys.

**The Time Corridor**

Begin this journey by asking people to imagine that they are walking down a wooded path. Invite them to enlist all their senses in order to really soak up the experience of being in a forested environment. (As indicated many times, if clients aren't visual, sensing, feeling or simply intuiting that they're in a forest is perfectly fine. In fact, feeling these realities can carry more impact than actually seeing them.) After being one with everything they're experiencing in this natural setting, offer that they turn down an imaginary fork in the road. Ask them to notice anything about this road that draws them, and suggest that as they walk slowly forward they'll soon see a building. Invite them to notice in any way that draws them, what the building looks like, how big it is, what the architectural design is, any feelings they might have in being there, or anything else that occurs to them. Then as they approach the building, suggest that they'll notice a short staircase leading to a large wooden door.

As they now climb the stairs to approach the door, invite them to notice or imagine what it looks like. Is it simple or are there ornate designs on it? What kind of wood is it constructed of? Then ask the client to state within the journey space that they wish entrance to the building. In asking permission, it's important to state specific intentions such as, "I wish to enter so that I can access a past life that will help me, or is specifically connected with, the issue (state the issue) that's troubling me in my current life." The door usually opens at this point, but let people know that if it doesn't open on its own they can simply go up to and open the door themselves.

Suggest that the space inside may be a long and narrow corridor. Along each wall they will notice a long bookshelf going down the hall, both shelves filled with objects. Suggest that they move down the hallway, seeing, sensing or intuiting as many objects as they can, until one draws their complete attention. Invite them to pick up and hold this object. They should notice how they feel in doing so. As they do, propose that they allow themselves to be drawn into the object; they'll be magnetized to merge with it. Once they feel fully one with the object they hold, the room around them will swirl and fade away as the object takes them into the distant past. In this past, they will arrive to a scene in a person's life that likely holds significance to your client's current life patterns. Remind the journeyer at this time that any of the events they see, sense or intuit will have already happened, and they should try not to become emotionally involved with them.

Allow clients time to experience the part of the lifetime the object induces them to recall. At a prearranged signal the person will let you know when they've completed their task within the journey (usually raising one hand or forearm). Once the journey is finished, they are to allow the past life scene to fade away and imagine being back in the *Time Corridor*. They can replace the object still in their hand on the shelf where they found it, return to the door and leave the building. Before they leave, they should express their gratitude for the experience. Allow them some time to walk back down the road and return to the forest. When among the trees, suggest that they take some time for nature to renew and replenish them before they imagine the forest itself fading away. When they're completely ready, they are to return to their body and come fully into the room.

## The Circle of Earth

Invite clients to imagine lifting up from the Shamanic Reiki table, drifting through the roof of the building and high into the sky. They are to continue ascending until they see, sense or intuit the earth spinning beneath them. Have them experience the continents as they appear and disappear in the turning of the planet, in whatever way comes to them. After experiencing the world turning a few times, invite the person to state the following: "Take me to the place and time that will help me understand the problem I'm facing now." (Or state this the same way as in the above journey or something else along these same lines.) Imply that they will now feel themselves being pulled down toward the earth.

When their descent slows, they may find one of several things has happened. They may find themselves in another body and experiencing another life as if it's happening to them now. If that is the case, invite them to look down at their bodies and feet to notice what they're wearing and from what time period their clothing and footwear are from. Or they may find they are whom they are in the present time, but hovering over and watching an event from another lifetime as it happens.

Or they may experience something completely different. It's important not to censor or judge what's seen, sensed or intuited. And again, whether the scenario is real or not doesn't matter, their experience and any information about the energetic pattern they are working to shift is the important thing. Trust that your clients will receive exactly what's needed at this moment. Allow plenty of time for them to immerse in the journey, and again, they should signal when it's complete. At this point they should allow the alternate reality to fade around them, and imagine returning to the sky while experiencing the continents below. When their home continent appears, they are to feel themselves floating down, back to the city they live in, back through the roof and then the ceiling in the room, and fully into their bodies.

### The River of Time

To get a sense of this journey, imagine that the first time your soul incarnates it's placed in a basket on the swiftly flowing *River of Time* and will continue to float down stream for as many lifetimes as your soul incarnates.

In this journey, your client's immediate goal is to focus on being at the edge of the *River of Time*. There, they will see (imagine, sense or intuit) an abandoned canoe along one of the banks. Suggest they get into the canoe and push off. The canoe will now begin to move up river, back in time. Once the canoe leaves the shore, have your client state the same thing as in the above two journeys. Anything along the lines of, "Spirit, take me to a past time when the problem I am dealing with now was first created." The exact words aren't as important as the intention. When the canoe moves toward a shoreline, invite clients to climb out of it and walk away from the river until they come to a person. They can take a moment to notice what this person looks feels and acts like. They should follow them until witnessing an experience this person has lived through. After the experience is over, people should withdraw from it alone to return to the canoe. The canoe will move downstream this time, and when it stops, they will have returned to the present time. Clients can then leave the river and return to the room and fully into their bodies.

Using one of these three journeys, one you've evolved on your own, or a technique you draw from your healing basket, you must facilitate a journey that helps the people you work with witness an event from their past, another lifetime. The significance of the occurrence visited is that it's one which negatively impacts them in this reality, this lifetime. But remember, the fuel that fires shamanic journeying is the intention of the journeyer. In the above journeys, the intention is to return to a past life in order to engage the energy and gain further understanding or resolve for a current problem. However, by changing the intent, your client can also use any of these journeys to access the more recent past to shift the energy of an issue created in this lifetime. Conceivably, you can also use them to access the future, shifting the energy of events that have yet to happen, which impact us now.

**Session Notes for Past Life Journeys**
As with all the shamanic excursions presented in this book, begin these journeys after channeling Reiki long enough so that your client enters a deep state of relaxation. During this time you can shapeshift into the energy of your Shamanic Reiki spirit guide, inviting them to guide the session for the highest good. You can also, at the beginning of any of the three journeys, suggest that the person can elicit the help or company of a spirit guide, if they have one, as they embark on their journey. Or, if they don't have a spirit guide, you can invite them to take anything along with them, an ally or helper, whatever energy, symbol, tool, animal or person evokes strength, healing, clear seeing and guidance. Or simply begin the way you have when initiating other journeys. As clients journey, with permission rest your Shamanic Reiki hands over their eyes and forehead to assist them in accessing other times and places. Or rest your hands wherever they're drawn.

As in traveling to the past to prevent soul loss and shifting the energy of past events, for Level Two Reiki practitioners and above, the absentee and mental/emotional symbols hold special significance for past-life work. By invoking the absentee symbol, we render the past, whether from this life or others, very accessible and send Reiki directly to the circumstances of the event, which is impacting our current lifetime. Through the mental/emotional symbol, we direct Reiki energy to accomplish core emotional and thought pattern healing of the past life circumstances affecting us in this life. The master symbol amplifies the power and addresses fragmentation of the soul.

It's important to note that simply witnessing and engaging the energy of a past life through any of the journeys above can prompt healing, or a spontaneous shifting of the energy of past events. This can happen before even addressing how to use what's gleaned from experiencing these stories or past lives. Although not the goal at this stage of journeying, stay open to the unexpected. Energetically sensitive or tuned-in people are especially prone to unprompted turn of events during the journeying process.

When our client suffering from abandonment issues traveled to a past life during the Black Plague, she witnessed her child-self at that time as a young boy hidden away in his family home. Before they became ill themselves, his parents had stockpiled food and forbade the child to leave the house despite what happened to them, as most of the village was afflicted. Now, the boy's parents had died, the food had run out, and the child was starving. But something unexpected happened as our client viewed these circumstances. Her attention, via the young boy, focused on a rat in the corner of the room. As woman and boy watched the rat, it suddenly transformed into a ball of light. This light then rose up through the roof and into the sky, the child's and woman's consciousness traveling up with it. The client experiencing the journey assumed this symbolized that the child had contracted the Plague and died also, its spirit ascending from the body. But in looking down from the sky upon the village, the young boy and the current-day woman saw a light emanating from within the surrounding forest. Both woman and child then traveled back down the light beam and into the house. The boy immediately ran out of the building and into the forest toward the light, in the direction viewed from the sky. He eventually reached a blazing cooking fire and a small community of survivors who took him in as their own. This is a good example of a spontaneous shifting of the energy of past events. Please note that this occurred when simply journeying to view a past life or energetic template to retrieve information.

Whatever the nature of their journey, when clients have completed it you can continue channeling Reiki. Feel free also to employ any Shamanic Reiki methods you're inspired to incorporate. Do so long enough to give time for the energies and experiences to settle, understanding that a rendezvous into the far past can deeply affect all levels of being. Then, when the moment feels right, you can invite the person you're working with to share whatever they're drawn to about their experience, or what insights they've gained. Or you can complete the entire session, saving this discussion for the close of your time together. Either way, this sharing is a time to clarify how the story relates to the issue, and what the person may now be inspired to do about it.

**Using Past Life Information**

Unfortunately, we can't tell you exactly how to use or interpret information and experiences particular to each client. We can give you an example, of course, tailored to fit the scenarios we've outlined. But by this time, you should trust that whatever's presented will spur in you the creative and intuitive wisdom needed to benefit your clients. And remember that the intention is what guides the process, so be clear about yours, and also the abundance of help that's available to you now, such as guidance from your own spirit allies. People may be skeptical about the process. Or they may feel the information's too good a fit, and therefore, must be entirely made-up. Assure them that believing or not believing isn't the issue, past life or not. Regardless of the origin, the journey will display the energetic template of the issue's root cause. Shamanism is very practical: the results are what matter. Our measure of success is the increased health and well-being of our clients.

After the death of the medical doctor's young patient he was devastated and never practiced medicine again. His aversion to the profession carried into a future life. Once this story was accessed, a second journey was taken to the past life to heal the wound. We've discussed journeys to the past to remove attachments from people who may no longer be alive, journeys to remove energetic connections to past events, and journeys to prevent soul loss. In each, clients dialogue with someone, another or younger self, to achieve the goal. The same thing can be done to loosen energetic attachments to past life incidents.

In taking this second journey, the person stated their intent to witness the previous life at the moment the young child died at the hand of the physician. As the child's life waned, our client focused attention on the doctor, looking for the soul part leaving his body and which caused this wound to perpetuate into another life. Ingrained in this disassociation was aversion to the medical profession. This is the part the person must dialogue with, yet with perfect hindsight. Yes, the child died, but in asking the physician why he chose to become a doctor in the first place, he can be reminded of those he's helped through the years and the lives he did save. This conversation also details the wonderful things that can happen in a future life, but explaining that the negative association to the medical profession will be carried on for more than a hundred years, harming them into the future. When the dialogue feels complete, the person invites the disassociated aspect of the doctor's soul and the physician himself to travel high into the heavens to a universal source of light. As the two rise and meet that light, they merge and the energetic link between our client and their far past will be dissolved.

Our role in this journey is most importantly to clarify its purpose to our clients. Once the intent is clear, to resolve the past life issue or an energetic template that's holding them back, they'll do just that, resulting in a shift of energy that accelerates healing. It is not always this pat and simple, though. In fact, it can take several journeys to convince a past-life piece to accept what the future person is telling them, to let go of the pain, and move into the light source. Yet after one or a couple of journeys, there is the potential for healing.

As examples of the results of such work, the woman, whose Black Plague journey spontaneously resolved when (as a boy) she found community and safety in the forest, now knew why she had such angst around relationship and separation. Because of this she gained more compassion for her issues and they felt more approachable. This client's panic attacks lessened and she began to practice what she learned in the journey of rising above painful situations to see them from a higher perspective. She applied these insights to relationships, letting go of unhealthy connections, trusting that she would find more nurturing ones. The person averse to the medical profession became less reactive and channeled energy instead into advocating holistic approaches to healing.

The wisdom, power and energy we gain from past life journeying can shift the ways we're negatively affected in this lifetime. We can unlock the chains of what's holding us back and in doing so not only remove its link to the current lifetime, but also to future ones.

CHAPTER TEN

# CREATING A SACRED CONTAINER FOR YOUR WORK

You've arrived at a foundational topic for this book, one we've saved for later in your reading so it stays ingrained and fresh. This is a chapter you'll want to return to over and over as its significance cannot be overlooked. In Chapter Two, we said, "In any healing session, regardless of the modality, there are three physical components: the client, the practitioner and the environment" and "When the three basic components of a healing session are harmonious, acting as one, miracles can happen." A sacred, consciously created space harmonizes client, practitioner and environment, opening the door to spirit.

This usually begins by tending the room or physical space, clearing this space energetically, and inviting healing powers to work through us for the benefit of our clients. Yet, there are also many other facets to the practitioner-client relationship and the setting we create around this, including the healer's inner environment and self-awareness. We may all know someone who's disliked a doctor's bedside manner, stopped seeing a healer or therapist because it wasn't the right fit, been turned off by a workshop presenter's ego, or some similar scenario. No matter how comfortable the physical space or how good the treatment, skills or message, the energy and attitude of the person delivering it has an affect. Whether acknowledged or not, everything occurs within a holistic environment. Subtleties like colors, sounds, smells, and even a person's energy and mindset impact us. In becoming aware of these factors, we can consciously cultivate a container of well-being and genuine relationship. No matter what the modality is, a true healing milieu includes, yet also goes far beyond, the observable interactions between practitioner and client, the actual physical space, and approaches used.

In the following pages we'll outline some of what we feel are the essentials for creating a sacred container for your work, some of which may already be nestled into your healing basket. We'll also share less recognized ingredients for empowering conscious environment. Feel free to place what resonates into your own basket, or adapt our suggestions to suit your unique style.

**Tending the Physical Space**

Most healers intuitively know how to create a space for their clients that's safe, relaxing and conducive to deep healing. Our physical healing space is our biggest asset, a powerful container that supports and sets the tone for our work. In theory it's true that we don't need special environments to perform Reiki, but in creating them, Reiki practitioners invite a richer experience for their clients. And Shamanic Reiki requires a protected space to access imaginative realms, especially for new journeyers. Also, as some journeys can be difficult, the practitioner should do whatever possible to make these experiences gentle. The primary way to do this is by making the physical session space safe and nurturing. Whether we conduct sessions in an office, a room in our home dedicated to healing, or in the living room if running our practice from our apartment, we must create sacred space.

The first step is to make sure the healing room is physically clean and fresh. Furniture and objects should be free from dust, windows cleaned, and the space tidy. Some practitioners like to clean their walls once a month with water and a bit of sea salt to keep them clear of energetic, as well as physical debris. Just as energy flows through the human body, clutter and grime impede the energy flowing through a room. A friend tells the story of an energy adept staying in his home. The host left for work early one day, with no time to clean up after their breakfast together. When he returned home the young visitor was standing in the living room wildly waving his arms and uttering incantations. Looking very pleased with himself, he announced that he had just cleansed the home. This perplexed his host who saw the dirty dishes were still piled high on the kitchen counter. The host wondered how this seasoned energy worker could miss the basics. Settling chaos in the physical environment is fundamental to clearing its energy.

Our mind and emotions reflect what's around us. With proper care and attention, our environments can help our clients feel relaxed and open. There are other basic parameters that can ensure this for session times. Turning off the phone ringer and locking the door eliminates unexpected intrusions. We've heard stories about healers constantly interrupting a session, the dog needed to go out, the phone rang, the dog needed to come back in. This can be agitating and make people feel unsafe. The client is the primary focus, so any personal business left unfinished before they arrive should be put aside, and all environmental factors should be settled beforehand to eliminate distraction.

The lighting should be soft, just bright enough to see clearly. We look into our client's eyes so that we can read the person's face, energy and body language. We set a gentle tone. Lowering the shades and partially closing the blinds allows a diffused light source. If there's room, have two comfortable chairs facing each other where you and your client can sit before and after the session. Remember to have fresh drinking water and tissues within reach. Be aware that sitting behind a desk creates an unconscious barrier, and sitting in a chair much higher or bigger than the client's subliminally suggests that we wield the power. We are in equal relationship with our clients. The practitioner has specialized skills for which a person offers an exchange of energy, usually in the form of goods or money. However, the ultimate relationship lies between the client and the spiritual forces the practitioner mediates, guided by the client's higher self. Our physical environment should reflect and support these values.

The décor of the room is of course, personal choice. Decorate and use color consciously. Remember that colors influence us psychologically, emotionally and physically as they can stimulate, depress, relax, agitate or accelerate healing. Many good sources are available for assessing the sway of color or you can consult a Feng Shui practitioner. Better yet, take a shamanic journey in the room before you go out to buy paint and furniture, and ask the space itself how to maximize its healing benefit for clients and what colors and overall feeling tones are best. Or journey to your existing healing space and ask what changes or shifts it suggests to better support your work.

Ever walk into a building and feel its character? Or after living in a home for many years, start to notice its distinct personality? Houses, buildings and rooms embody living energy we can communicate and participate with. When John Perkins brought several indigenous Shuar shamans to New York City on their first trip out of the Amazon basin, he thought the massive city would overwhelm them. John was stunned when one man went up to a sky scraper and pressed his hands against the concrete, connecting with its energy. He told John that perhaps our culture has too many buildings, but as they are here, they require our attention and gratitude. It shocked this shaman who had witnessed North Americans hugging trees in his rainforest homelands, to see us ignore the spirit of our own buildings and homes.

In the journey space, by meditating or simply tuning into the room, ask to connect with the spirit of your healing space. Intend that you'll receive guidance in any form it comes regarding how to create a sacred healing environment. It may be in the journey as ideas and images, in a dream later that night, or as an unexpected gift for the space. It may come as a casual suggestion from a friend dropping by. You may be shown where to put furniture or the practice table, which colors to use, or special items that should be brought into the room to induce calmness, awaken the senses and attract healing forces. Renew your connection with the spirit of the healing room each time a client comes to you. You can also ask if any additional item wants to come into the room for a particular person. Trust the guidance you receive. Don't censor it just because you don't understand it. For instance, if you connect with a stuffed teddy bear that's hidden away in the attic, assume there's a good reason for it. Ask the space to love and support your client's journey. Be sure to thank the space after your client leaves when the session is done. You'll feel the energy of the room begin to glow the more you tend to, appreciate and engage it.

Even if you see clients in a tiny living room or a cubical you've rented in the city, make the space as protected, supportive and wakeful as you can. Connect with and show appreciation for the spirit of your healing space whatever its size or content, intending sacredness for your work.

One of our students evolved her Shamanic Reiki practice from humble beginnings. Until she could afford a professional practice table to work on, this woman met with her clients in her kitchen, placing a decorative futon on top of her breakfast table and using that as her Shamanic Reiki table. In such cases, anything that suggests that this is the time and space for your client's transformation and healing has a powerful effect. We can transport any area into a sacred container, even an ordinary kitchen. Whatever the environment, it should aid the client in leaving preoccupations behind and becoming fully present, so they can actively engage in the healing process.

## Sanctifying the Space

If you must keep your healing room simple, remember that the main ingredients to set and maintain the tone are your intention and state of being. Coupled with the right intent and awareness, a single candle, a special stone or a bouquet of flowers may be all that's physically needed to evoke sacredness. A single lighted candle can summon the energy of the five elements: earth is represented by the solid stick, air by the rising heated currents of air over the flame, fire by the flame itself, water is represented by the liquid wax, and spirit is the light that radiates from the flame. Burning one candle honors and evokes the five elements, inviting their presence and healing influence to awaken in your healing space. If drawn, when lighting the candle, affirm in a whisper that each element is present, infusing power and guidance throughout the session.

If the space is reserved for healing alone and big enough to set up a small altar, water fountain or similar focal point invoking the presence of the elements, that's ideal but not essential. Objects in the room should awaken the senses, calm the mind, and communicate appreciation and beauty. Ecuadorian Andean shamans taught us that the beauty of the flowers rubbed onto the client's body during cleansings, and the fragrance of the aromatic waters rubbed onto their skin magnetize healing spirits. Tibetan teacher, Chogyam Trungpa Rinpoche, instructed about the magic of *dralas* saying that dralas are natural, wakeful forces that can be engaged in nature or an interior space. Invisible to most of us, dralas are living energies drawn to beauty and cleanliness, and which interact with us when we're attentive, present, and appreciative. Cleanse and beautify the environment, then through simple prayer or invocation express your gratitude for the living, wakeful energies of the space. You may feel noticeably clear and sense the abundance of spiritual help available for your work.

As mentioned earlier in the text, before the session you'll want to fill a glass or ceramic bowl with sea-salt water and place it near or under the Shamanic Reiki table. If your healing room is rural or near a park or natural space, you can also go outside to collect tree branches for your work. See what healthy tree calls to you. One in particular may offer itself for healing sessions, but remember to connect with the spirit of the tree before cutting its branches. A simple way to do this is to first look at the tree, noticing its physical details and beauty. Let awe and reverence for the living natural world pervade your body, heart and senses. Then you might want to place your forehead or palms against the trunk, sensing its energy and life force. Let mind and body relax. Be one with the tree, if even for just a moment. Then ask its permission to collect three branches for the person coming to see you. When you sense the tree's permission, hold a Reiki hand just above where you'll take a branch, where the cut will be made. When the time feels right, with your other hand simply snip the branch. As you do so, feel and express your gratitude for the offering. You can also leave a little bread, flower petals or loose tobacco.

You may want to walk the land briefly before sessions, to ground, focus and feel your gratitude. You can make offerings to the land and waters, inviting their participation. Take the time to acknowledge nature as the larger sacred circle holding and supporting your work. If you're in the city, there is still the land, trees and sky to connect with that surround and support your building, as well as the building itself. Feel the power and healing energies of the natural world flowing through and activating within you. When back inside, place the branches on your altar, or on a special cloth on a table, within easy grasp for the session. You'll also want rattle, drum, feathers, crystals, sacred stones, flowers, or any items you desire to have on hand, within reach. Remember that your client can go outside to offer the used branches and flowers back to the earth when their session is done. (Items gleaned from nature and other natural items like flowers are only used for one person and one healing session.) Cleanse other items in the sea salt water or place them in sunlight to clear and re-energize.

Energetic and spiritual healers often scent their healing rooms by placing a few drops of an essential oil, such as lavender or clary sage (relaxants), in a dish of water over a candle diffuser, or burn incense such as frankincense and myrrh (offers protection and opens the veils between worlds). Similarly, shamanic practitioners often *smudge* the room or their clients, lighting a small plant bundle then blowing it out, so the smoke can clear stagnant energies and magnetize helping spirits. Tibetan and Siberian shamans may use juniper for clearing and ceremony, others use sage, sweet grass, cedar or aromatic woods. But since many people are allergic to essential oils, incense, smoke and scents, we ask ahead about sensitivities. One solution is to open the windows and smudge or scent the room before people arrive so the smells mostly dissolve before the session.

Reiki Level Two practitioners and above can evoke the Reiki symbols in the space to empower it before sessions by visualizing them in the space or drawing them in the air with their hand. An alternative shamanic approach is to blow with the breath of spirit, camaying the symbols into the space. This can be done by drawing the symbols in front of you with your hand or visualizing them, then with a forceful breath, blowing through them, seeing, knowing or feeling their energy pervade the room. Plant your feet firmly, feeling your connection with the earth before you camay, feeling spirit's power infuse your breath as you mindfully blow toward the symbols.

Other ways to ensure an energetically brilliant space, if not smudging, using essential oils or incense, are to amplify it through sound vibration. Drum or rattle, ring bells or chimes, clap your hands or chant. Each has distinct effects and vibrations. You can combine them, use one after the

other, or use those that call to be used for specific clients or circumstances. Quiet, unobtrusive methods just as effective in clearing the space
before your client arrives are to open all the windows and let the fresh air
and sunshine pour through the room, or to visualize brilliant light
pervading the space. You can also waft a feather through the room to clear
and disperse energy, lightly mist every part of the space with sea salt
water (plant misters work well), or dip white flower heads into consecrated water then flick them, sprinkling the room.

This last approach combines the gentle vibration of the flowers with
the cleansing element of water. Our students consecrate water by setting
a glass or ceramic bowl of well, spring, stream or rain water outside or on
an inside window sill under a starlit sky, or for the three nights before a
full moon. The water absorbs the star and moon vibrations. This is a great
way to integrate full moon energies and the star or moon water can be
used ceremonially, for healing work, or to enliven a space. Reiki Level
Two practitioners and above also draw or visualize the Reiki symbols in
the water, or summon the symbols in the air just above the bowl, then
blow them into the star or moon water. A variation comes from a student
who created a *moon garden*. In addition to using star and moon water, this
woman planted multitudes of white flowers that glow under the celestial
night skies. When they are saturated by star or moonlight, she picks those
that call to be used for consecrating and healing.

Regardless of the method, set and maintain your intention while
clearing and illuminating the space. Don't forget the floor and ceiling
corners where energy accumulates and gets dense. Visualize, feel, or just
know the mode you're using is clearing stagnation, energetic clutter and
debris, and filling the space with sparkling, sanctified energy. If you're
stirred to move or dance through the space, follow the impulse. We
synchronize mind and body and shift our own and the energy of the space
around us through mindful movement in consonance with larger spiritual
forces. These can powerfully express through our body and voice. When
facilitating large workshops, we often get people up to dance or playfully
move around the room to keep the energy of the space, and everyone in
it, grounded and expansive. Don't think about what you're doing, just

follow the urge, trust and enjoy it. If a chant, prayer or words come to you, voice them or sing your decree to activate sacred space. You may channel wisdom from other times and places.

Be sure to crack a window or door open when energetically clearing, especially if smudging, so the dense energy has an exit route. Or visualize a Reiki energy vortex, a universal life force energy spiral, in the center of the room that continuously sweeps disharmonious energies up and out of the room and through the ceiling and roof. You can intend this spiral to be in place throughout the session, dissolving the form when the session's done. Don't have a thought as to where the discordant energy is going, or that it could cause harm elsewhere. Energy isn't inherently bad as everything is illumined at its source. Whatever flows into the Reiki spiral is immediately transmuted and recycled into the universal life force. You, and the room, will become warm-hearted and bright as you move through the process.

Over time and in playing with these methods and immersing in Reiki, our healing rooms and we become attuned to higher, lighter vibrations. In merging with these forces, our ecstatic shamanic knowing is roused. Then it becomes easier to evoke sacred space on the spot.

**Music and Spirit Guides**

Playing soft, meditative music is calming, relaxing and helps people move more into their bodies and emotions. There are powerful audio tools for healers including music to synchronize brain hemispheres, clear and activate the energy centers or chakras, and nature sounds reverberating elemental forces through the room and into the client's physical and energy bodies. There are also shamanic drumming CDs and music designed for shamanic journeying. You'll find resources and suggestions at the end of this book. Music can be played throughout the session including during discussions, so it remains a subtle, potent backdrop. When the physical and energetic qualities of the room resonate, clients slip easily into a receptive mode. The goal is to help them open to whatever occurs throughout your time together.

After creating your healing environment, stay relaxed and grounded to be a clear conduit for spirit and Reiki. Your intention is to create a clarified container for the work, channel beneficial energies for your client, then release the rest to spirit. Forget about the outcome. Whatever happens is supposed to happen. Spirit gives us what we need, often in surprising ways and for reasons we'll never understand. This may not be what a client is looking for at the time, so we must be supportive regardless of the outcome. We can't any more take credit for a spontaneous healing than we can feel responsible for what's perceived as an unsatisfactory outcome. The practitioner is only the intermediary. Healing unfolds in the perfect timing and circumstances that spirit and our client's higher self direct. There are never negative aspects to sessions and it's important to embrace that whatever occurs happens for a reason, despite our ability to understand it.

As we walk the shamanic path and deepen our relationship with Reiki and Shamanic Reiki guides (please refer to Chapter Seven), we can establish a host of relationships with non-physical guides and teachers. Some become more important than others as they strike a deeper chord in us. Nothing occurs in a vacuum and integrating spiritual helpers into the concept of sacred space empowers us and our work.

The wonderful thing about calling in guides is that once we do so, they're with us throughout the session, so we can ask for their help at anytime. We may feel them as a tangible vibration, or experience goose bumps or tingling sensations as we feel them come into the space. We ask them to guide the process for the higher good of our client and we can call upon them in whatever way or manner seems right.

Similar to the way we become one with Reiki as it channels through us, we can merge with our Shamanic Reiki guides. The simplest way to do this is to visualize our guide as one with us, really sensing its energy. We invite the guide to direct its energy through us during the session, for our client's highest benefit. When the work is done, we thank our guides and release them.

In working with clients over time we can also evoke their own spirit helpers, or invite them to do this. Some seek Shamanic Reiki to resolve specific issues or during crisis, yet others come regularly as an overall strategy to stay clear, healthy and spiritually aligned. Clients we know more intimately may share those images, people, animals or items that evoke healing and transformation for them. Or we can facilitate a shamanic journey for them to discover their guides.

## Giving Form to the Container

In a Shamanic Reiki session, the healer-client relationship is sacred and confidential. Boundaries can get a bad rap, yet ignoring them sets the stage for chaos and mistrust. We don't talk about what happens in a session outside of it, something we make explicit from the first meeting. This allows those we serve to relax, become more open about what's really happening for them, and engage the healer-client relationship genuinely.

It's also best to be clear about session times and what exchange we're asking. As we see people for extended times and interact creatively with spirit and in nature, we never commit to closing on the exact minute of any hour. We indicate that the session begins at a specific time and ends within a half hour range, say between 3.00 and 3.30. We're flexible, but clear. Picture the best boundaries as those that offer form, yet breathe with the life they're intended to accentuate and nurture. With less ambiguity, there's less confusion. Clients are reassured in knowing what to expect.

We've all heard of healers who say no one should receive an exchange for spiritual work. Yet in Reiki healing and shamanism, exchange not only helps clients value and take responsibility for their healing, it represents a vital and reciprocal flow of energy. Energy coming in has to be balanced with energy offered out. The contribution is for the spirits and healing forces, which the healer facilitates access to. The practitioner receives compensation for this, and their time. We can punctuate this relationship by having clients place the exchange on an altar or near sacred items. As they do, they express gratitude for spirit's work on their behalf. In later collecting this from the altar, the practitioner symbolically receives it from spirit.

Exchange comes in many forms and shamanic Andean peoples are even offered live chickens, a traditional gift to the spirits of the land, sacred springs and volcanoes. For our own sessions accepting live chickens doesn't work, so sliding fee scales make healing available to everyone despite cash flow. When comfortable in doing so, bartering for services and goods frees us from the monetary system and honors the creativity and skills of community members.

Creating a conscious container for sessions is as important as cleaning the physical space. Another aspect is the flow of the session itself. Most relevant is the beginning and ending. Healers exclusively focusing on table work don't realize the effects or opportunity of what comes before and after. How present we can be, how deep the work goes, how grounded our clients are at the end of a session, how smoothly they'll integrate things once they leave, all are reinforced by clear beginnings and endings.

Some practitioners begin sessions with relaxed breathing then sit in silent meditation with their clients. This aligns the two and settles mental and physical energies. Practitioners can tune in psychically at this time by being fully present to what they notice, feel and sense. They can also call in, or shapeshift into, Shamanic Reiki guides. Clients can call in their own spirit guides, or whatever evokes healing, comfort and power for them. This time of silence can be profound and emotions can bubble to the surface, accelerating the work that follows. Before or after this, drawing from a spiritual card deck can reflect what's most present for clients. These can be placed under the Shamanic Reiki table during the session. The candle ritual and/or the *Cleansing with the Elements* journey (both in Chapter Five) can also be done in this beginning time. Opening in these ways makes conversation more connected and useful, the work richer.

In closing, clients need transition time. After you lift the last Reiki hand, gently touch their shoulder and whisper that you'll be back in ten minutes. This allows them to return from alternate reality in their own manner. Let them know to take the time to come fully back into this reality before slowly sitting up. The music should continue playing. Bring a fresh glass of water back with you and ask them to drink it when sitting upright. They can close their eyes as they drink, imagining the water as liquid healing light soothing them internally.

The energy field expands during Shamanic Reiki and people differ in how much time is needed to integrate these shifts. If they seem spacey, make sure they don't get into their car until fully grounded. Make eye contact, rub their feet to bring their energy into the body and have them connect with the earth. Placing a cleansed rock in each palm can be helpful and boji stones work well. Get them to crawl around on the floor with you if they seem disoriented. Gently rubbing the back across from the heart area protects and gently seals the energy here, a place that's commonly vulnerable after emotional work. Sharing should be conscious and client-driven, yet being in silence together first is advised. Sitting up after an energy session is like waking from a dream; the experience is more textured when we take our time and apply tender awareness.

In closing a session we make ourselves available, if something unexpected comes up and the person needs us after they leave our healing space. We suggest they take a walk in the fresh country air or around the block before heading home. This is a good time to offer to the earth any plants used in the session, feeling their gratitude for what's been received.

## The Inner Environment of the Practitioner

Despite mountains of suggestions for creating a safe and sacred container for Shamanic Reiki, the one thing you should go away with is this: ultimately everything is sacred. The chickens that walk in and out of the shaman's healing space are as sacred as the ancient Incan stones that adorn his altar. We can create powerful healing spaces as described above, but in tending to someone needing our help on a busy street corner or in a frenzied hospital setting, we can evoke sacredness on the spot. Our most potent healing tools are our intent and state of being.

How do we cultivate a presence that can settle chaos, evoke sacredness, and radiate compassion in any situation under any circum- stance? There are many ways. Naropa University (Boulder, CO) psychology graduate students ground therapeutic work in meditation and body-mind practices. The programs emphasize that our own state of being has a profound impact on others and is the basis for any healing relationship. We're in sympathetic rapport with the world, influencing and being influenced by everything around us. Good midwives make the most of this by indulging big, expressive yawns in the presence of laboring mothers to help them stay relaxed and open.

In creating a sacred container for our work, we can't overlook the impact of our own energy. We don't have to be perfect, yet we do have to be present. In doing so, we make room for the person we're working with to do the same. This is an invisible practice that's healing in itself and it's amazing how quickly people pick up on how present we are. Just as Shamanic Reiki practitioners read energy, clients read a practitioner's movement, speech and breathing. They intuitively know to what depths we've suffered, what we've healed, and what we've swept under the carpet.

Practicing Reiki healing also helps us evoke sacredness on the spot. In channeling and merging with the universal life force, we attune to higher states, open our hearts, and become more present. This awakens us to an expanded way of being, and not just when we're practicing Reiki. We begin to understand that nothing's separate from the universal consciousness and that sacredness is ever present, always accessible. We only have to intend it, to recognize this.

Beyond meditating, developing a relationship with our spirit guides and the elements, and doing Reiki, we can cultivate a healing presence before people arrive for sessions, stay present with someone needing our help on a public street corner or flood a chaotic hospital environment with sacred, healing energy through the following practice.

The practice we call *Light Breathing* has variations in many cultures. It helps us open our hearts and stay grounded, yet expansive. Regular practice makes these effects easy to initiate and radiate at anytime. Light Breathing is a tool for becoming fully present, and for emanating sacred forces that can benefit others.

**Preparing to Practice Light Breathing**
Find a comfortable place to sit for a while where you won't be disturbed. Take some time to stretch and release any tension from your body. Then sit and breathe for a few moments at a normal pace and rhythm. Have the intention to let go of preoccupations and distraction. Take some time to

simply be.

As you sit, notice the feeling of the breath as it moves in and out of your body. Feel the sensations of air on your nostrils and lips and the movement of the breath through your body, noticing the rhythm of your breath. Is it smooth and spacious as a spring breeze, or is it choppy or cut off at the chest? Bring your attention to the qualities of your breath without judging or trying to change anything. Breathe this way for a while, simply noticing.

After some time, allow the breath to relax and deepen, breathing all the way into your lower belly. Soften your belly and lower back so the breath can move fully into this area, allowing the belly to expand out naturally with each in-breath. The belly fills with air first, and then the air rises into and fills the chest and lungs. The out-breath fully releases at its own pace. Breathe fully into your whole body now, allowing the breath to penetrate every aspect of you: bones, tissues, ligaments, muscles, cells, organs, emotions, thoughts, spirit. Shoulders are dropped, relaxed, and your mouth is slightly open relaxing jaw and hips.

As you breathe, feel the firm contact of your body against the floor and feel the connection with the earth beneath you. Feel the heaviness and weighted-ness of your body and the nurturance, support and healing energy of the earth. At the same time, sense the space all around you in the room, then the space outside the room, beyond the walls and roof, out to the trees, sky and beyond. Feel this in your body, remaining fully in the room. Continue breathing in a relaxed manner at your own pace, feeling the simple rhythm of your breath.

Remember that you can always come back to the rhythm of your breath. This can invigorate the body, bring space and alertness to a busy mind, and help to integrate emotions. When the breath is smooth and full the mind relaxes and the senses awaken, we feel things more richly and have abundant energy. The breath oxygenates the blood, releases toxins and aligns us to gross physical rhythms in our bodies such as the flow of our blood and beat of our hearts. As well, it connects us to energy rhythms in our bodies, to subtle earth and cosmic energies.

**Practicing Light Breathing**

From here, the instructions are simple. As you breathe out, remain present and fully in your body and in the room. Yet at the same time, extend your consciousness out with the breath, releasing with it anything that's ready to go, such as tension, worry, pain, constriction or confusion. Just let it go. Feel your awareness extend to the far expanses of the universe, to the far horizon, or expel the breath deep into the earth if you prefer. Expand your awareness out with the breath, yet stay with the feelings in your body. Stay fully present in the room. Feel yourself as part of the vast space all around you, and at the same time, remaining fully in the here and now.

On this exhalation open to collecting and retrieving luminous, sparkling, healing light in these vast spaces. You will bring this healing energy all the way back to you on the next in-breath. Breathe this life force in through your nose and mouth with your breath, but feel it also penetrate every pore of your body, 360 degrees around you. Feel this light infusing and replenishing every cell, muscle, organ, bone, tendon, tissue as well as emotion, mind and spirit. Feel the light nourishing, revitalizing and energizing you.

Continue the *Light Breathing* practice at your own pace until you are filled with light. You may have palpable sensations of this light cascading through you. On each out-breath you expand out, releasing whatever needs to go. With each in-breath you collect and retrieve brilliant life force energy – abundant in the vast expanses of space all around you or from the earth, and breathe this nourishment back to vitalize every part of you and your body. Stay centered and fully embodied. You are not ejecting *out* of your body with the breath, but embodying fully, expanding *into* your essence qualities.

Continue for five minutes or so allowing the sensations and life force to grow within you. The light radiates beyond the bounds of your physical body now, into the space around you. You emanate healing light. You don't have to strategize this energy, only know that it pours forth from all around you and is particularly concentrated in your heart and hands.

Allow some time, then gently let the practice and sensations dissolve. Return to a normal pattern of breathing. It's ideal to go out and take a walk to integrate the energies. Walk mindfully, noticing how you feel.

*Light Breathing* attunes us to universal light. This is not the polarized light of *light versus dark*, but the non-dual ground or essence quality of everything. The practice helps us become clear conduits for spirit and radiate sacred conscious energy to others and the environment. It can also be taught as a healing tool for clients and regular practice makes it easy to do on the spot. Once you're well practiced at it, the effects are simple to summon whenever needed. Even in a hectic hospital room or busy street corner, upon thinking of the practice you can immediately connect with the energy and clarity of this light, as well as radiate it out. It will become automatic and available simply through your intention.

# CHAPTER ELEVEN

# SHAMANIC REIKI ABSENTEE HEALING

By now you should be unequivocal about accepting from this book what resonates with your unique path as a Shamanic Reiki practitioner whose primary guidance derives from spirit. Our goal has been to offer a creative repertoire of healing approaches that empowers your work beyond technique. It's especially important to keep this in mind as you read this chapter, as long-distance healing requires personal adaptation and a clear alliance with spirit. Instead of repeating this throughout the following pages, we'll say it succinctly now. Take in what you read, alter or incorporate it in ways that are harmonious for you and your clients, and remember that it's the intention that directs the energy.

Absentee or long-distance healing is just what its name implies, in this case offering Shamanic Reiki despite client and practitioner not being in the same room together. There's no limit to how far apart the two can be. We've practiced absentee healing for years and it works every time, whether clients are one or many thousands of miles away. Energy readings are astoundingly accurate and we see positive results despite never meeting the person we're working with. How is this possible? Spirit and Reiki energy transcend location, time and space. The universal life force is non-dual by nature and not restricted by laws that govern a three dimensional reality. It can move back through time and even leap into the future. In shamanic world view this is represented through the concept of oneness. We are interconnected through time and space by luminous filaments of energy and just as the internet is a web of communication, this living web of light informs and connects all of sentient life. (This is an unconditional, more intrinsic level of connection than the dependent or even the beneficial luminous cords mentioned in Chapter Three.) With clear intention we can reach any person, time or place. We can access information and draw energy to us via these light filaments and as well, we can extend healing energy and compassion out to others through them.

Absentee healing takes many forms and crosses diverse cultural and religious boundaries. Most of us routinely extend healing energy as this can be as simple as whispering a prayer for our children, projecting comfort when driving by the scene of an accident, sending positive thoughts to a college student taking an exam, or radiating hope to tragedy victims halfway around the world. Instead of trying to explain the phenomenon we'll share examples. But the best validation for absentee healing will be gained through your own practice of it and in witnessing its results.

Many years ago Brazilian shaman Ipupiara Makunaiman gave a shamanic workshop at Misty Meadows Center in Lee, New Hampshire. One morning he initiated a group meditation to access healing energy offered by a shaman friend in Peru. The participants circled together, held hands and closed their eyes. Ipupiara walked through the room chanting softly as the 23 people opened to the Peruvian shaman's energy. Within a short period of time one group member began to shake. Her body soon vibrated so forcefully that Ipupiara stopped chanting and asked for help to lay her on the floor. The participants gathered around the person, covered her with a blanket and propped a pillow under her head. Ipupiara asked that they place their hands on the woman's body to balance the powerful forces channeling through her from Peru. This person was simply the focal point or conduit for energy intended to reach the whole group. Many placed their hands on the woman until her shaking finally subsided. After opening her eyes, she described traveling in alternate reality to an indigenous woman dressed in colorful garb and chanting a haunting melody. The sounds elicited palpable energy that flowed into the group member's heart and the warm, blissful sensations still radiated through the woman's body. The participants felt this force emanate from her. They said it was like being enveloped by love.

## Absentee Healing and Reiki

For shamans as well as Reiki Level Two practitioners and above, healing and transferring beneficial energy at a distance is a common practice. We have other stories and absentee approaches to share, but before getting into more specifics we'll address a few issues.

First, since absentee healing is traditionally taught in only Reiki Level Two trainings one might wonder how a Reiki Level One person can participate in what's presented here. We do advise getting attuned to Level Two so you can be empowered to apply symbols directing Reiki energy across time and space. But, as shamans and many other healing and spiritual practitioners send energy at a distance without using the Reiki symbols, you can do this too. Reiki Level Two practitioners open absentee healings with symbols intended to send energy at a distance. Reiki Level One folks can focus on the shamanic aspects of absentee work, yet begin sessions by asking Reiki to charge their healing space and guide the distant healing. They can then do Reiki on themselves and journey to the Reiki energy to merge with it (see Chapter Seven) and ask it to infuse their work. The *Light Breathing* practice from the previous chapter is also a great tool to infuse self and space with the universal life force.

Second, since this is not a Reiki handbook we won't elaborate on how to use the long-distance symbol or describe techniques Reiki masters may teach for performing long-distance healings. Reiki Level Two practitioners and above already know how to send Reiki across time and space so they can incorporate this part of the absentee session into the description below. As we've done throughout this book, we'll offer ways to integrate shamanic approaches within Reiki healing.

**Setting up Absentee Sessions**

People seek absentee sessions for the same reasons they might pursue in-person healings: for support through life changes and when confronting physical issues or navigating life-threatening illness; to stay balanced and relaxed; for insight on specific problems and important decisions; to clear emotional baggage and release undesirable patterns; for spiritual growth; to improve relationships; to empower life purpose and direction, and so on. Despite any commonalities, the individuals, circumstances and outcomes are always unique.

Working long distance offers a special and intimate relationship whose benefits can last weeks, months, even years. Similar to the way we conduct in-person work, a Shamanic Reiki absentee session is an intensive healing package requiring the client's full participation. We discourage less than six months between sessions unless there are special circumstances. This way people can utilize the tools, insights and practices we offer to help them effect the changes they desire and to anchor the energetic shifts the work initiated. Clients may choose to receive support through this time through long-distance phone coaching.

Absentee sessions are set up in advance and to facilitate our connection clients provide us with several things before we begin the work. We typically describe the healing process through email and provide a list of the items needed and where to mail them (office or post office box). The most significant article clients send is their photograph. We ask that no one else be in the picture so we're not distracted when looking at it or picking up someone else's energy. We prefer full body shots because the way bodies are shaped and held, as well as the person's expressions and background environments, convey so much. Along with the photo, people send us a few strands of their hair, a short sample of hand-writing on a piece of paper (writing anything that inspires them), a small article of natural fiber clothing they've recently worn (flammable material and something they don't need back like a tee-shirt). They should also include the exchange amount asked for the work.

Shamans believe people radiate personal energy that permeates their clothing, jewelry, car or house keys, and other items. Individual energy can be read through such items and also accessed through a bit of the person's hair, carried through the vibration of their name and through their photograph. For this reason, those traveling thousands of miles to work with shamans in remote locations can leave disappointed if they desired to return home with pictures of their indigenous teachers. Many shamans don't want their energy accessed through their image. On the same token, they can give astonishingly exact readings from photographs of others and use them, or pieces of clothing, to extend healing energy to those unable to make the trip abroad. Intention alone is enough to send energy where it's needed. But using items imbued with personal energy gives a concrete focus and offers easy entry to the energy field.

After the items arrive we email the client to schedule a 10-minute phone call. We provide the number and the person calls us at a designated time. In preparation for this conversation we invite the person we're working with to reflect on what's most present for them, what's most on their heart. The call begins with a few moments of silence when both practitioner and client take some deep breaths, relax body and mind, and allow external distractions to settle. Practitioners can go to their sacred place, intend for the highest good of their client, and shapeshift into the energy of a Shamanic Reiki guide so this presence can pilot the exchange. Or they can simply set the intention for the highest good of their client, breathe, relax and become present. Reiki Level Two practitioners and above may evoke the long-distance and other symbols, as well as project Reiki to the person at the other end of the phone.

This call is about connecting, establishing trust, inviting our guidance to work in consonance with the person's higher self, and strengthening our energetic link. It isn't about gathering information. Although we may hear specifics about our client's situation, presenting problems and symptoms are often secondary to root causes. To facilitate a deeper exchange we ask people not to worry about what they'll say but to simply open, relax and speak from the heart. Astute practitioners listen compassionately yet wakefully beyond story line and surface issues. To do this we stay present, engage our senses and open our hearts. We tend to the quality and sound of the person's voice and its effect on our emotions and bodily sensations. We notice what images or insights pop up for us as they speak. Intuition is indispensable for working across time and space and with it, the trust that what's needed will arise. We remind clients and ourselves that most significant in this conversation is what occurs beneath, between and through the words. As we listen and offer what inspires us, we hold our client in a space of unconditional positive regard.

Some practitioners coordinate session times with absentee clients so that regardless of where they are, the person receiving the healing can participate. In this case, the practitioner may ask about the environment the person will be in at the time they do the session so they can imagine it clearly. They'll invite them to meditate, reflect on pressing issues, lie down and take a shamanic journey, or just remain aware and open during the appointment time. Obviously, time zone differences have to be factored in. Reiki Level Two practitioners and above may also do distant sessions this way, invoking the Reiki and absentee symbols and then sending the energy out to the person. Or practitioners may conduct full Reiki or Shamanic Reiki sessions during this pre-arranged time, imagining and summoning the energy of the person or by using a surrogate.

Our own approach acknowledges time and space as illusion and empowers clients in other ways. We let people know we'll perform the absentee healing session within two weeks of the initial 10-minute phone call. Instead of setting a pre-arranged time, we do the healing when we're guided to do it which also gives us the option of working in stages. We intend and trust that the energy will impact our clients at the optimal time and in the most favorable way. We release any ideas or expectations of when or how that will unfold.

Our clients have prepared, in part, by collecting and sending us the absentee items. We also provide them with instructions for *Cleansing with the Elements* and the candle ritual that we begin in-person sessions with. The more active a role a person can take in their healing, the better. We emphasize the power of their intention to heal and change, which galvanized when they contacted us. We explain about the precursory healing energies that are now activated and how to maximize the benefits of this *portal of opportunity* (journaling, paying attention to dreams and synchronicities, etc. – see Chapter Two). We agree to email our clients sometime before the close of two weeks when the work is complete, in order to set up another phone call. We schedule 45 minutes to an hour for this final sharing.

## Preparing for an Absentee Healing Session
The previous chapter detailed the importance of creating sacred space for Shamanic Reiki and absentee healing doesn't preclude the necessity of

this. In fact, because client and practitioner aren't physically close to each other, setting the space can be even more important. Please refer back to Chapter Ten, since the environment you create must be able to hold your attention, intent, and protect the work from impact by other energies. And as powerful as creating external sacred space is, you also must cultivate and project sacredness from within. Do this by settling into your body, resting your mind, opening your heart and merging with the universal life force and Shamanic Reiki guides. Then to radiate this energy, trust your intuition and stay clear. Again, the *Light Breathing* practice is a powerful vehicle as is establishing a Reiki energy spiral in the room. You can also walk outside before the session to center, ground and connect with the sacred circle of spirits and nature as for in-person healings. This is a good time to express gratitude, make offerings to the land and collect evergreen or other branches for the healing work.

After preparing self and the space and before beginning, make sure you have everything needed to perform the absentee healing: shamanic tools such as flowers and/or plants, frame drum and beater or a rattle, bells and feathers if drawn, a glass of water, a lit white candle, smudge item and matches if desired, your client's postal mailed items laid out on a special cloth on the floor or in front of your altar, a notepad and pen to record journeys and information during the session and whatever else nudges you to be included.

Open as you do for any Reiki or long-distance Reiki session for Level Two practitioners and above, or as indicated in the above section called *Absentee Healing and Reiki*. With palms extended out, beam Reiki energy at the photograph for a few moments as you repeat the person's name three times and invoke their presence. Then just relax, open your heart and gaze at the photo. Don't think or work too hard, allowing insights to come naturally. Intend that you'll see, intuit or sense only what's helpful to your work. Many describe this type of reading as *opening the third eye center*, located approximately in the middle of the forehead. This is a powerful and natural practice yet one that must be grounded in compassion and non-attachment. We don't force inner seeing to happen, just intend it and it occurs. Keep a pen in hand and the notepad nearby so you can record any insights. If you feel that stopping the session to take notes would be distracting, you can speak into a tape recorder during your session. (Most useful are those that only record when you are actually talking.) Then go through the same process with the hair, article of clothing and sample of handwriting. See what emerges, pay attention to bodily sensations, hunches and feelings. In closing your eyes while holding the object, images may appear or your guides may whisper to you.

Let the process flow and don't work too hard for information or to make sense of it all right away. Take some deep breaths and relax into body and environment, releasing expectations and outcome. Beyond what's perceived, connecting energetically this way deepens the work that follows.

You can also pick an animal card or use any other type of spiritual card deck at the beginning or end of this process. Shuffle the deck and say the client's name three times while visualizing the person clearly in your mind's eye, or simply feel or intend their presence. You can invoke the Reiki symbols over the cards if at Level Two or above, and Level One practitioners can hold the deck in their hands asking Reiki to infuse it. Hold the intention that the card chosen will mirror what underlies your client's circumstances, then cut the stack and see what card lies at the bottom of those you've lifted, or fan the cards out and select the one that calls to you. The card or animal indicates the archetypal allies supporting your client at this time. You can then keep this card with the client's materials so its energies will be present throughout the healing session. For this reason, we usually select the card in the beginning. The totem also reveals the spiritual lesson and growth opportunities inherent in the person's current life situation. Take notes on what insights, associations or intuitions come to you beyond the author's explanation for the card. Later, you'll share these with your client so they can elicit this archetypal support on their own.

### Absentee Shamanic Reiki Journeying
From here, there are many ways to proceed and one of the first is to

embark on a shamanic journey. You can sit up or lie down during your journey while holding and beating a frame drum or a shaking a rattle. Or you can play a drumming CD to guide you. Level Two practitioners and above can project the Reiki symbols into the journeying space, and Reiki Level One practitioners can simply intend for Reiki energy to infuse the journey realm. Then visualize, feel or intend your client's presence in the midst of this loving, protected space. Render the person as clearly as possible.

Now, feel the presence of or shapeshift into your Shamanic Reiki guide, asking to be shown what more you need to see, experience or know about the person you're working with. The information can come as images, feelings, symbols, metaphors, literal information or through stories. For instance, your client may suddenly be swaying gaily on a swing or you may sense ghost-like figures surrounding the person. Don't censor the material because it's bizarre or doesn't make sense. From a rational point of view you're working "blind" at this stage, so just relax and trust the process. Remember that spirit is the director and can see quite well. Allow yourself to become comfortable in not understanding everything and the work will flow unobstructed with powerful outcome. You'll understand more as you proceed, with some pieces taking time to clarify. But they are exactly right, so trust that all progresses for your client's highest benefit.

You can complete this exercise then close the journey. Or you can proceed within the journey space to the spiritual healing technique described below. See what feels right and honor the impulse. As spirit has its own agenda intensive healing work may begin with the first drumbeat. Alternate reality is mutable, energetic and efficient so what most needs to happen will come to the forefront. Surrender and trust is essential. The journey may last 15 or 55 minutes. During the informational process we may intermittently stop to take notes or continue until the journey's finished, saving note-taking for later. Or we may do separate journeys, conducting the work in stages.

## Spiritual Healing Work in the Journey Space

Spiritual healing during the journeying process can be performed from two equally valid perspectives, one entirely spirit directed and spontaneous, the other a strategically applied shamanic procedure. Core areas are addressed, energies are balanced, soul pieces can spontaneously realign, intrusions can be removed and transmuted, and blockages cleared through spiritual healing in the journey space. The work focuses in areas the practitioner identifies within the shamanic journey or from the initial phone call, or the journey is completely guided by spirit.

**Approach One** In the exclusively spirit-guided approach, you begin the shamanic journey with two intentions: 1) first to see, sense, intuit or know whatever more is needed about this client and 2) then to invite spirit to do whatever healing is needed in alternate reality.

After the first phase of the journey is complete, in visualizing the person you may see spirit guides and benevolent beings working with the client: balancing energies, removing obstructions and energetic cords, rousing energy in some areas and smoothing it in others. Light beings may dialogue with the person and remove dark or sharp objects from them as well as place stones or crystals into their spiritual body. Alternatively, light or luminous energies may be directed into the person you're visualizing. You may perceive one or more of the elements participating in the healing, similar to the *Cleansing with the Elements* journey. These can manifest in a myriad of ways, such as your client being cleansed by a cascading waterfall or purified by standing in a roaring fire, etc. You may see one or several colors swirling around or through the person and also see yourself in spirit form doing the work instead of, or alongside, spirit guides. Animal guides may appear as well, such as an animal ally from the spiritual card deck or any other number of things.

As you watch or sense the healing, you may experience heightened body sensations like tingling, warmth and increased energy. You may sense, see or spontaneously know the issues being addressed and to what and whom they're related. You may witness the client releasing emotion in the journey space, such as through sobbing, ranting or screaming.

Any number of things may happen in spirit-directed healing work and it's different every time as well as for every person. As practitioner you simply set the intention for spirit to orchestrate the work that will most benefit your client and trust the person is positively impacted. Then hold the space as a sacred witness. When the spiritual work is complete the guides and helping energies disperse and heightened bodily sensations relax. The client's spiritual form is radiant or clear and the person seems peaceful and happy. They may appear to stand at the center of the Reiki spiral you've invoked in the room. When this phase of the work is over, close the journey and record the details.

**Approach Two** The strategically applied shamanic procedure sometimes called *spiritual surgery* is particularly effective for physical problems. You also begin the shamanic journey with two intentions although the second one is different from that of the spirit-directed work: 1) to see, sense, intuit or know whatever more is needed about this client and 2) to see, sense or intuit imbalances that you will work to balance within the spiritual realm.

After the first phase of the journey is complete, in visualizing the person you'll imagine entering their physical body and traversing through them to detect "imbalances" in any area. If there's a specific issue you've learned about from your client such as leg pain, go directly there or where your intuition says the problem originates. In spiritual reality, it's not necessary to understand what's sensed, only what area in our client's body needs attention. This area may be dark or seen as an impediment like a wall or fence enclosing the person's heart or other organs. You may intuit a blocked artery or a bone with barbs attached to it.

What's sensed isn't as important as how you feel about it. When you have a clear feeling of heaviness, stagnancy or imbalance in a certain area stay there and invoke the assistance of your Shamanic Reiki guides. First, with the help of your guide, you may communicate with the form asking why it's there, where it came from and what the person can do to prevent its return once removed. You'll share these insights with your client on the final phone call. There aren't any hard and fast rules except to do whatever makes the area appear healthier. Your guides may whisper instructions or conduct the work through you. You may imagine holding a hammer and chisel and chipping barbs off the bone or see a deluge of water flushing out a clogged vein. You may dig out each fence post barricading an organ, and as you remove it, ask your guide to take it (as well as the sludge from the artery or barbs from the bone) out of the client's body. Or you may toss it into the Reiki spiral in the center of the room to be recycled into cosmic energy. Trust your impulse and just as you sensed the imbalances in this area, sense or see when the area feels right, clear and healthy.

At this juncture, from within the journey, intend Reiki to permeate the area of the body where you worked. Since this is spiritual reality you may even see the Reiki energy. At the exact time you're sending Reiki from within the absentee session journey, from your healing space or office, Level Two practitioners and above can concentrate on the long-distance symbol, directing energy to the client. This way the person receives Reiki energy simultaneously within both spiritual and ordinary realities. Reiki One practitioners will only send Reiki within the journey. When you feel finished in one area, yet sense something in another area, continue journeying through the body to find it. If the work feels complete, gently withdraw your consciousness from the person's body, close the journey and return to ordinary awareness.

This type of spiritual healing is common to many traditions and for a deeper discussion of it we suggest reading Michael Harner's *Way of the Shaman*. Please note that throughout this book are many other examples of journeys you can take for absentee clients: shifting the energy of past events, soul loss prevention, past life journeying, etc.

## Absentee Cleansing with the Elements

After journeying, we cleanse with the elements to integrate the spiritual healing/surgery. (If doing the healing in stages, we may do this cleansing at another time.) Laid out in front of us are our client's hair, photo and piece of paper with handwriting sample set on top of, or alongside, their tee-shirt or other clothing article. These items rest on a larger cloth used for absentee healings only, concentrating the energy and protecting the underlying surface. We have shamanic tools within reach: feathers, plants, flowers, water, stones, smudge items or incense as well as drums, bells, rattles and any other items. The white candle still burns brightly. We play a drumming CD or chant to heighten awareness or we do the cleansing in silence. Similar to working with the elements in-person (refer back to Chapter Five) we do the same via the objects carrying our client's energy.

Open as for any Shamanic Reiki session (or absentee for Level Two and above), shapeshifting into your Shamanic Reiki guides. Then see what elements call and how they want to be used. Intend for your guides and tools to conduct the work through you. Say your client's name three times as you invoke their presence for the cleansing, feeling their presence through the items spread before you.

Then you may smudge, drum and camay water directly onto the objects. You can grasp a plant or flower bundle, wipe it over the tee-shirt to cleanse the person then tap a gentle rhythm feeling the plant transmit healing energy to the person you're working with. Holding stones, you might click them together over the photograph then rub them on the article of clothing. In doing so, feel the strength and power of the stones infusing your client, and with it voice any sounds that arise. Intentions must be clear, heart and body engaged. Feeling, moving and voicing will help you channel effectively and increase empathic awareness. Brisk movement, waving, chanting, grunting and blowing, all characteristic of Quechua shamanic healing, intensify and move the energy. They also open intuition. The more present and engaged you are, the more powerful the energy.

Try wafting a feather over the items to smooth the energy of the person, similar to smoothing the energy with your hands at the end of a Reiki session. Ringing several clear tones of a Tibetan bell, or chiming over the articles, seals the work you've done. In closing your absentee session, you can deepen your client's connection to the universal life force through the practice outlined below.

## Radiating Healing Light

As in sending Reiki energy at a distance, this practice transmits luminous healing energy to any location and time. If you don't have articles, visualize or sense the person or situation in front of you. Or write the name on a piece of paper and focus energy there. You can also direct your intention toward the Reiki energy spiral in the center of the room asking the vortex to send healing light where it's needed.

**Practice One** Sit comfortably with your client's absentee healing items spread before you, feeling the person's presence as clearly as you can. Do the *Light Breathing* practice as introduced in the last chapter until you feel grounded, present and one with the source of healing light. After several minutes and when you feel saturated with light, allow this force to radiate from and all around you. Keep breathing light in and as this light pools within and all around you, intend for it to also be directed to, and to infuse, your client. Visualize, feel or sense this light penetrating the items before you and permeating the person whose energy they hold. Continue practicing this way for several minutes and let the focus gently dissolve. Take several deep cleansing breaths and return to a normal breathing pattern.

**Practice Two** Begin as per above and practice *Light Breathing* for several minutes. This practice raises your vibration, rendering you resilient to invasive energy. It also grounds and strengthens your ability to transmit and radiate healing energy.

Now, bring the practice to a close and envision the source of this luminous healing light. You may see it high above you as a ball of Reiki energy, described earlier in this book. If a Level Two Reiki practitioner, you may envision this luminous source of energy as a violet or gold light encasing the Reiki symbols and hovering high in the heavens or vast cosmic spaces. Or notice what comes to you, or just sense the light without an image. Feel the loving intention and the indestructible quality of this light. When you have a firm sense of this light and its location, intend to access and direct it to benefit your client.

Reach up with both arms to feel and collect energy from this light source. When your hands are full of light and on the next in-breath, breathe this light down through the top of your head. Guide it into your crown with your hands, then continue moving your hands down as you guide this light through your throat area and into your heart. (As this light source isn't separate from us anyway, an alternative approach is to shapeshift into it.) From here, on an out-breath, beam the luminous energy out from your heart. Direct it to the image of the person in front of you or to the absentee articles. If desired, use your arms to help propel the energy, pushing them out with palms facing what you're projecting the healing forces to. Make a strong "shhhhoooo!" sound as you expel the breath and transfer the energy. Feel, see or sense this healing light flow to and infuse the person you're working with. Repeat the sending practice for several cycles then relax. You, the healing space and your client should feel luminous and clear.

Illustrating the power of these practices is a story about a Dream Change training group that learned about a boy who was hospitalized after a brutal beating. The young man was having seizures, his EEG was grim and his family braced for the worst. The Dream Change folks sent healing energy to the boy and his family – a nine-hour drive away – through shamanic techniques. Upon their altar lay a piece of paper with the child's name on it. They directed energy there, as well as sending it to the boy via the Reiki vortex in the center of the room. The parents reported back in a few days to say the doctors cited their son's recovery as no less than *miraculous*. Most intriguing was that the most recent test results totally differed from the documentation describing his first EEG – and that the initial EEG itself was now mysteriously missing. The day before the group sent energy to the teenager, they also placed the name of the ageing father of one of the participants on their altar. The man, who was considered gravely ill, stabilized by the end of that day then rapidly improved. Though it can't be proven that the group had any real influence on these people, their families were convinced they had a phenomenal impact.

## Closing the Work

Again, we encourage you to incorporate traditional Reiki absentee approaches into the above format in whatever timing or way feels right to you. Upon completing the long-distance session, offer the used plants and waters to the earth and express gratitude to the elements and helping spirits. Cleanse stones or crystals in sea salt water, and then set them and the other shamanic tools in the sun to recharge. Return the handwriting sample and bit of hair to an envelope addressed to your client and drop it in the mail. Burn the tee-shirt and photograph in an outside fire-pit, fireplace or woodstove. In doing so, ask the fire to fortify the healing for the person and to transmute any residual energy. If you live in a city and can't burn the items, hold a lit candle near them and invoke the same intentions. Then return these materials to your client. Sense how to cleanse the space. Feel what it needs by being guided by suggestions in Chapter Ten.

You'll want to notify your client that the session is complete and set up the final phone conversation. Gather and review your notes before the call and follow the instructions above as in beginning the initial phone contact. From here no one can say exactly how to proceed but some basic areas need addressing. The client should know the hair and writing sample are on their way (and perhaps the photo and tee-shirt) and that these items hold no negative energy. The person is to create a simple ceremony to burn the hair and paper, fortifying the healing with intention. If the tee-shirt and photo have also been returned, the client can burn these as well or place them on an altar or in a special location. The objects now generate healing energy and are tangible reminders of new life directions. The client also offers bread, flower petals or loose tobacco to the earth in gratitude to the elements and spirit helpers. The candle ritual has already been done, but after the final call the person can light a new candle for one evening, meditating on the new life door that's been opened through the work. In sitting with the candle and journeying into this doorway they may view what allies, changes and actions will help sustain the shifts they've experienced.

Practitioners share the card chosen, the work done, as well as journeys, details on spiritual healing and surgery, insights and intuitions. The material is also provided in writing, mailing or emailing it to the client as soon as possible after the last phone call. We ask spirit and Reiki to guide us to share in the manner and timing that will most benefit our clients. People are encouraged to contribute their own insights and to reflect on what the material evokes for them. Much is revealed, new information may flow for the practitioner in the process and previously *blind* areas may resolve themselves. For instance, the woman who was depicted on a swing in the journey space had taken trapeze lessons in her twenties. The fearlessness this brought out at that time had supported her through a tough period of change. She now recognized the need to reconnect with those qualities to navigate current challenges.

Adding long-distance healing to your healing basket includes a powerful element that can be used for new clients that can't travel to you, or existing ones whose circumstances prevent them from physically returning to your healing space. When the latter is the case the person's energy can be accessed simply through holding the client in memory.

To close, we repeat that intent is everything, the prime mover in both shamanism and Reiki. By opening your heart and maintaining clear focus and intention, energy directed at a distance will be strong and effective. It will travel exactly where it's needed and exert its influence in the perfect timing and manner, regardless of the physical location of your client. In trusting spirit and self, and engaging the person you're working with in empowering healing rituals, long-distance healing can be as powerful as working with someone lying on the table in front of you.

# CHAPTER TWELVE

# TRANSFORMING SELF AND WORLD

Arriving at the final chapter of this book we trust that by now you recognize Shamanic Reiki's potential to improve the quality of a person's life. Each modality, shamanism or Reiki stands alone as a powerful agent for healing and change. When combined, the practice coaxes us to look deeply within ourselves and engenders an active interplay with spirit and life-giving forces. Shamanic Reiki can help people heal and feel connected to the living world.

Throughout this book we've stressed that in shamanism there are no steadfast rules. What works for you, even if it's something unique to your practice, can be as valid as what's worked for a shaman halfway across the world through the course of that shaman's lifetime. Given enough time, your trust and connection to spirit will grow as will your ability to personalize the techniques in this text and intuit new approaches.

When the first humans thousands of years ago followed spirit's whisper in the form of a vision, dream, synchronous event or intuition to find the right shelter, animals to hunt, or plants for healing, they integrated the material and spiritual worlds. Acknowledged or not, spiritual reality does exist and interfaces with all of our physical reality. The guides we've spoken of, the spirits of the plants, elements and shamanic tools, along with the cosmic and earthly forces, are incessantly around and within us. We need simply open to and engage with them. Using shamanic journeys and working with the elements, our intuition and Shamanic Reiki spirit guides can help resolve resistant issues and make us feel more whole and alive. In becoming more familiar with the processes, you'll experience firsthand why shamans access spiritual realms and archetypal forces for healing. Retrieving power, wisdom and energy from other worlds to benefit the people or circumstances of this world will become a reliable course of action.

## Shamanic Reiki Empathic Awareness

We've emphasized throughout these pages that opening heart, body and mind will increase personal awareness and attune you more closely to spirit's nudge. As mentioned in Chapter Ten, we're in continuous empathic exchange with everything around us, a concept that can be consciously applied in healing sessions. When an unexpected or seemingly extraneous idea, feeling or body sensation arises for a Shamanic Reiki practitioner during a session, the origin of the experience may be related to the person lying on the table in front of them. By harmonizing with the life force energy and the spiritual world, practitioners can act to positively affect the physical, emotional and mental states of the person they're working with.

Cultivating an empathic exchange by observing whether our thoughts, emotions and bodily vibrations reflect what's occurring for others can be an efficient healing strategy. We can refine our intuition to help us gain insights that logic may not point to in terms of how to best help our clients. For example, while channeling Reiki we may notice our chest suddenly tighten and our breathing become choppy. From this, we could intuit our symptoms to reflect an energy constriction in our client's heart or lungs.

One means of loosening the blockage would be to consciously relax our own body and breathing, empathically transmitting ease and fluidity to the person we're working with. If our mind begins to race, one thought after the other, and this isn't the norm for us during a healing session, we might intuit our heightened mental activity to reflect our client's state of mind. Again, we consciously relax our body and breathe comfortably. Then, in asking the Reiki energy flowing through us to help release our thoughts into space with each breath out, we calm our own as well as our client's mind. Watching people visibly relax as we hold this silent dialogue with the energy is awe inspiring. The key is its simplicity. By attuning to ourselves, we open a door that allows us to connect on a deeper level with our clients. In adjusting our own energy, altering our own state of being, we can empathetically communicate love, healing and peace to the person we're working with.

Through the course of these pages we've suggested many challenging journeys that you may decide to navigate with your client. By developing empathic awareness, you can help your clients without interrupting their journey. In another simple example of how to employ empathic exchange, imagine that while the person is journeying back to alter the energy of a past event, you suddenly feel very sad. Knowing that it may be mirroring your client's experience, you can gently move a Reiki hand over their heart. Or you can simply ask the Reiki energy to flow through your own heart before leaving your body and entering your client. When your own feeling of sadness either takes on a richer quality or dissipates, you can assume that it may also be transforming for your client.

Remaining present, focused and connected to spirit helps practitioners differentiate their own personal issues from their client's. Healers can cultivate this awareness by doing their own therapeutic work, becoming mindful through practicing Reiki or meditation, and through peer and other supervision processes. In addition to being a healing agent, being alert to and clearing our own energy is essential for empathically sensitive people. If we're not sure that what we're experiencing has anything to do with our client, we still stay conscious of, and work with, our own experience. Shamanic Reiki practitioners are aware that their own state of being profoundly impacts, and is in continuous rapport with, that of their clients as well as everything around them.

**Empathic Exchange and Balance with Nature**
Similar to our empathic relationship with clients, we're also in a continuous sympathetic liaison with nature. Yet through the centuries, dominant members of the human species have persistently tried to move us away from a sensitive coexistence with the natural world by exploiting the environment to suit material goals. To substantiate this, all we need to do is look at the number of species that have become extinct in the last hundred years, or look at photographs from space that document shrinking rainforests, toxic waters, and polar ice caps that are melting at a much faster pace than anyone anticipated.

It's not surprising to know that whether in Tibet, on the Siberian steppe, in the Amazon Basin or elsewhere, traditional peoples understood the importance of living harmoniously with nature. Based on our learning from indigenous tribes living in the Ecuadorian Amazon whose contact with the outside world is still minimal, we know that early shamans guided their communities to honor this relationship with nature. A shaman's role was not only that of a healer. Equally important was maintaining balance between their community, nature and the cosmos. Traditional Amazonian tribal peoples were sustained by shelter and food the rainforest provided. They were guided and healed by dreams, spirits, the medicinal qualities of plants, as well as the spiritual qualities of the elements, minerals, plants and animals. Attunement to natural forces and unseen reality was inseparable to stewarding ancestral forests, lands and waters, as both were an unquestioned fact of life for survival.

North Americans visiting Tuvan shamans on a Dream Change/Sacred Earth Network trip many years ago were transported in dilapidated army jeeps across vast expanses of the Siberian and Mongolian steppe. Escorted by police cars to deter marauding bandits, the small band went from village to village performing ceremonies and healings. As whole communities showed up for most events, the results of the Soviet regime were clear to see. There was alcoholism, poverty, depression, suicide, social degradation and disregard for the environment. Beyond individual healings, the Tuvan shamans attempted to mend the fragmented culture by reviving the villager's spiritual and earth honoring roots. Impassioned, fierce speeches began each ceremony urging people to care for the earth and not leave garbage on her. The villagers were warned that their problems would continue if they didn't steward their lands and waters, and respect the spirits through ceremony again. Maintaining balance with the earth and spiritual realms was the journey back to wholeness.

More than ever we're forced to understand that health, happiness and wholeness for the individual don't happen in a vacuum. An individual's stresses, struggles, emotional or health problems can't be viewed independently of their family, community, culture and environment. Given the high incidence of addictions, depression, stress and pollution related dis-eases in the US alone, it's not far flung to surmise that threatened ecosystems result from, as well as mirror and reinforce, the collective imbalance of our species. Separating from soul, spirit and nature causes suffering and depletion for all.

Healers are wise to follow traditional Amazonian and the Tuvans' example of not separating individual from communal, spiritual and planetary well-being. Remembering our oneness and staying balanced with nature also helps Shamanic Reiki practitioners become effective healers, as in doing so they gain smooth entry to the realm of intuition, a primary tool for healing.

In our modern day, compartmentalizing shamanism, Reiki or Shamanic Reiki as healing modalities dissociated from the environment is a mistake and missed opportunity. Nature is integral to alternate reality and inseparable from shamanic practice. Through intention and the practice of Shamanic Reiki, our exchange with nature heightens as does the awareness that the earth and we are one living system. With the knowledge that we are part of that same system, the necessity of caring for the earth and all who live upon her comes to the forefront. Along with this comes the recognition that we heal ourselves and help others heal in doing so.

Beyond being a healing form, Reiki also invites us to live in consonance with the universal life force, which goes hand in hand with being in right relationship to nature. Shamanic Reiki offers so much more than proficient healing or adding shamanic techniques to traditional Reiki. Through direct experience it can revitalize our relationship to the living world, entwining us with the very heart of nature and spirit.

## Rhythms of Healing, Transformation and Life

Everything in nature and in life carries rhythms. We physically experience some of these like the beat of our hearts, pulse of our own blood and the cadence of our breath. Beyond our body's rhythms are the rhythms of day and night, the change of seasons, the waxing and waning of the moon and the tides. There are also rhythms we may not be consciously aware of, as in the subtle energies flowing through us and within nature. Rhythms aren't always steady, but sometimes irregular tempos that can be soft or loud, strong or gentle, and which ebb and flow yet with consistent unfolding. A haphazardly flowing stream navigates huge boulders and bends in unpredictable and ever changing ways, yet unfailingly finds its destination.

From a shamanic point of view our rhythms are sympathetic to those all around us. Conscious birthing environments support the highest empathy between rhythms that are unique to each mother and child. In the healing process also, essential rhythms are supported between client, healer, the earth, spirit and the life force energy. These rhythms demand our full participation and presence. As we're one with the web of life, they invite us to heal, live and create with the breath of life itself. Reiki practitioners become highly attuned to energetic and life force rhythms and Shamanic Reiki practitioners expand this attunement to the natural, physical world. In doing so, we can harmonize with nature's innate living intelligence. Attuning in these ways can guide us through chaos and change, and transform us.

The prevailing values of western culture are material based and self serving. For the most part they consist of acquiring material goods, achieving success, money, social status and well-being for the individual or corporation. Inherent in this paradigm is the tendency to assess the worth of others by these standards, imposing them on the rest of the world. Living this way causes stress and disharmony for individuals and for the global community. It interrupts our alignment to natural rhythms which, in turn, limits our ability to access the living wisdom connecting us all. It's also in shocking contrast to traditional indigenous values that were centered on nature, community and family. Many Amazonian tribal peoples worked only three or four hours per day with plentiful time to play, for lovemaking, story telling and sharing dreams. Children were continuously with elders and parents learning how to hunt, gather and tend the plants, honor the earth and water goddesses so food was plentiful. It seems obvious that much of the stress we incur in our modern world reflects disconnection from more whole values that nurture life, happiness and unity.

Many healing practitioners are aware of this and try to live as harmoniously as possible with the world around them. By shifting our consciousness to embrace our oneness with life, our perceptions expand so we can more easily tune into nature's healing rhythms. In doing so, we better understand our place in the world and in receiving nurturance from nature, the earth and cosmic forces we remember our own and the universe's perfection. Additionally, each person has an inimitable healing path, as well as distinctive talents, skills, passions and temperaments waiting to be called forth. We can trust that the ideas and inspirations coming from deep attunement with the natural world are aligned with our own, and the earth's higher purpose. Actions that arise from such insights generate unity instead of disconnection.

We don't believe it's an accident that natural health care and energetic therapies proliferate in the modern world today. There are still conservative pockets that won't accept anything new and view what's outside their own orientation as radical. Despite this, Reiki is routinely offered as a complementary health care option in many North American hospitals for pre-operative and post-operative patients, for pain reduction, relaxation, and prompt healing. The practice of hatha yoga and eastern martial arts disciplines are integrated into the interdisciplinary health approaches of spas, fitness centers, medical institutions and gyms. Massage, acupuncture and meditation methods are mainstreamed and we don't view shamanism as that far behind.

Reaping health benefits from ancient traditions fits present day needs and its spiritual facets are food for our hungry souls. Although we're moving in the right direction and notwithstanding the many paybacks of holistic practices, they're often compartmentally inserted into systems that remain materially-oriented. We suggest there's another step to climb on our quest to live healthier and happier lives. That step requires that we shift our consciousness. We must recognize that no healing system or institution is truly holistic unless it acknowledges that the body, mind, emotions and spirit of humans are one with each other, the earth and all that thrives upon her. In harmonizing with the earth, we can reduce individual stress which is a powerful healing instrument. But from a Shamanic Reiki perspective, attunement and awareness of how local and global environmental issues impact us isn't enough to overcome modern stresses. Staying balanced in an imbalanced world is almost impossible as we're one with the larger whole. Each of us is responsible for contributing to and living in a manner that supports the vitality of all life on this planet, and consequently our own.

### Healers as Agents of Change
### Shamanic Reiki Community Healing Circles

Reiki masters and practitioners from myriad traditions and backgrounds mirror the shaman's role as agents of change. Reiki consciousness, energy and values are brought to the community level through Reiki Shares and Circles in monthly Reiki Healing Nights and Clinics, and other spiritual circles offering Reiki. People gathering in homes, bookstores, libraries, churches, hospitals, civic centers and elsewhere reconnect with spirit without religious dogma to mend body, mind and soul. Radiating the consciousness of oneness is a powerful tool in itself. But from a Shamanic Reiki perspective it's also important to concretely raise awareness of our interdependence with nature and the need to live harmoniously with her, to offer energy to people and situations beyond ourselves, and to harmonize with our living earth. This supports some of the changes in awareness we just spoke of.

The format below for a Shamanic Reiki Share or Circle holds deceptively simple power. Gatherings are open to the general public, fed by word of mouth and promoted by sponsoring locations. Facilitators may also circulate flyers and since no fee is charged for the circle, they can announce it for free in *community service* sections of local newspapers. We advertise the event plainly: *Community Healing Circle*. Gatherings typically run one night per month on an on-going basis, for instance, on the third Wednesday of every month for a two-hour block. Optional donations may be asked to cover any expenses.

Facilitators often have one or two partners and rotate leadership so the circle doesn't get bogged down by, or dependent upon, a single person. Other healing practitioners are invited to help the facilitators with the hands-on part of the evening. We've mostly worked with Reiki and

Shamanic Reiki practitioners, yet have also included Therapeutic Touch, Polarity Therapy/Reiki practitioners and others. This is a great vehicle to unite and support local healing groups. The number of practitioners is relative to how many folks are anticipated and it's better to have too many than too few. Yet as the energy is environmental, a ratio of one practitioner to about four or five participants is all that's needed, with more details on this below.

Things to have on hand for healing circles are: straight-backed chairs set close to each other in a circle with extra chairs on hand, adjustable lighting, calming background music and a CD player, a box or two of tissues, a small bell, a hand-sized huaca such as a stone (by now you know how to acquire and care for these) to be used exclusively for this circle, a decorative cloth, a pen and a small hard cover blank-paged book and a table set against the back wall of the room to place a mailing list sheet with a pen and brochures. You can include your own and other holistic resources, as well as those related to renewable energy technologies, shifting global paradigms, spiritual activism, spiritual ecology and more. (By clicking on the *Wakeful Organizations* link at www.dreamchange.org you'll find additional information.) You'll need a watch or clock that doesn't tick loudly to keep track of time, a single white candle if the sponsor permits, and a personal water bottle for the facilitator. You can also include a bouquet of flowers, some evergreen branches and/or a small bowl of consecrated water if inspired.

We don't scent the room or bring exotic spiritual or shamanic paraphernalia, only natural objects that transmit beauty, wakefulness and healing. We use unobtrusive means before people arrive to bring in the power of the elements and sanctify the space, such as those outlined in Chapter Ten. We don't promote beliefs beyond: 1) the living healing intelligence of nature and the universal life force, 2) oneness with the earth and the necessity of staying in balance with her, 3) the power that comes from being able to express ourselves genuinely in a supportive community setting. Everyone is welcomed, no matter what his or her orientation or background is.

The healing circle presented below is a time proven model, yet you may be inspired to alter it before placing it into your healing basket. If you do, keep in mind that once you settle into a form that works, it can be wise to stick to it. People open more easily when comfortable and knowing what to expect each time they come. The strength of the model builds over time and through repetition, so it's not long before the circle feels like it runs itself.

## Conducting the Community Healing Circle

People are encouraged to chat informally before the circle starts and a bell is struck gently 15 minutes before beginning. At this time we introduce the decorative blank-paged book, circulating it with the pen throughout the group. We explain that although we'll each receive healing this evening, many of us know someone who couldn't come, but is suffering. We're also all aware of global social and environmental issues, as well as the consciousness that perpetuates them, that need transmuting. We suggest extending beneficial energy to people and these situations through our intention. People are invited to write in the book, the first name and age of whoever they'd like to offer healing to. They may also write a few words describing a local or global situation in need. It's explained that as the energy is innately directed, it will impact each person and situation according to the highest good. If, or wherever the energy is not open to being received, it's simply absorbed into the earth or universal field. A variation of this would be to pass around a small basket and blank paper. Participants are encouraged to write the same information about people or situations they wish healing energy to be sent to and place the paper into the basket.

When completed, the facilitator places the closed book or basket in the middle of the circle on the floor on the decorative cloth. White flower petals can be strewn around the book and on the fabric. A single white candle lit or unlit, depending on what's sanctioned for the space, can be placed nearby. The evergreen branches can also be placed here next to or surrounding the water bowl, perhaps with white flower petals floating on the surface of the water. Or the center can simply hold the book or basket. The facilitator may privately visualize a vibrant Reiki energy vortex spiraling up from this focal point.

The bell is rung again, people are asked to take a seat and the lights are dimmed. A few chairs are left open for latecomers, less of an issue when there's social time built in at the beginning. The facilitator sits facing the entry (easier to welcome latecomers) and the other practitioners mix in amongst the participants. Music is playing and a box of tissues has been placed within the circle. The facilitator holds the stone huaca in hand.

The facilitator welcomes the group, introduces themselves and invites practitioners to stand so people know who they are. Then a general introduction ensues, beginning with a short explanation of what the universal life force energy is, how it's applied for hands-on healing and what people might expect in receiving it. The facilitator also explains about the concept of oneness, helping people understand that we can't ultimately separate personal from planetary wellness, or our own from that of the well-being of others.

Before passing the stone for sharing, encourage people to let outside distractions settle –they shouldn't be ruminating about the parking ticket they got that afternoon, for instance. The facilitators and practitioners are the conduits for, and maintain the integrity of the group. The more embodied and mindful they themselves are the better.

We describe the simple sharing exercise that begins the evening. The stone, holding healing intentions, will be passed to the left around the circle. As each person clasps the stone they briefly state whatever inspires, what's most present for them on a heart level. This can be a personal sharing or concerning a larger situation. For instance, one person may be dealing with life-threatening illness, another concerned about global warming, someone else may express the joys of being a grandmother, another may feel upset about the political and social state of the world, or someone might feel gratitude to be in the circle. Any expression is welcome with the only guidelines being to share from the heart and that only the person with the stone speaks. It's important for the facilitator to ask people to be brief, only sharing a sentence or two before passing the stone to the person on their left. Folks not drawn to verbalizing may hold the stone in hand or against their heart, perhaps closing their eyes and taking a moment to share from the heart in silence before passing the stone on.

People often later comment on the heat generated by the stone during the ceremony. It's made explicit that everything that occurs or is spoken within the circle is sacred and respected as confidential, not shared outside the room. When the container feels safe, complete strangers can open to one another in genuine, caring ways.

The sharing is followed by a five or so minute visualization experience led by the facilitator to help individuals relax and open before receiving Reiki. You can create one yourself on the spot or before the circle, or look for examples in holistic books or CDs. The main focus should be: to relax body and breath, open heart, body and mind to the universal life force and connect people with the earth. People are encouraged to close their eyes during this exercise and keep them closed throughout the healing touch that immediately follows. It's made clear that hands will be placed on the recipients' head, shoulders, upper chest and back only. They may feel warmth or tingling sensations while hands are touching them, and possibly also when not. We explain that the energy isn't limited to the person being touched, so even when not actively being worked on, they'll still receive energy. The sender and receiver's task is the same – open, relax and enjoy.

The healing portion lasts approximately 45 minutes, after which practitioners sit back down. If time permits, the stone is passed for a final sharing, conducted in the same way as above. The depths to which people may share at this point, the palpable energy that radiates from each person and the group as a whole, can be very moving. The facilitator thanks everyone and closes the circle. Time is reserved at the end for deeper discussion and community building, and light refreshments if the hosting space allows.

## Notes for Circle Facilitators and Practitioners
Although what's presented below is oriented to a *Community Healing Circle*, you might like to integrate some of the ideas into your general

healing practice.

The facilitator sets the tone for the evening, and as such should be the first to hold the stone and share. It takes awareness and practice to open personally while keeping the group's highest interest at the forefront. We gain support for this through the *Light Breathing* practice, by evoking the Reiki symbols, shapeshifting into Reiki and our Shamanic Reiki guides, asking Reiki to guide us or by simply setting a clear intention. Feedback from other facilitators and practitioners is invaluable. We don't need to be perfect presenters to run a public circle, but just to have a desire to help the world and be able to relax our egos. In fact, our own vulnerability and genuineness helps others feel less shy about being who they are. Again, with the right intentions and format, a healing circle will pretty much run itself.

Greet and relate with people warmly, make them comfortable and feel welcomed, connecting with them and connecting them to each other. Open your heart and in doing so, open the space for magic to happen. Don't forget humor and playfulness. Feel the spirits and the power of the elements with you. Even a stark room in a clinical setting can be transformed into a sacred, healing vessel with the right regard.

Ask people to open their hearts as sacred witnesses while others share, offering their silent attention. Quechua shamans in Ecuador perform individual healings for visiting North Americans with everyone in the group present, acknowledging the fortitude of community. Encourage feeling a connection to each person beyond appearance and words. The facilitator makes eye contact with each participant as they finish with the stone, or simply nods or whispers, "Thank you." We can't overestimate the value of authentic sharing and acknowledgement within community. Individuals can be so touched by the stone passing ceremony that they may cry. Slowing down, really listening and being heard, feeling the uncomplicated yet enchanted atmosphere of sacred space, is a rare and riveting experience for many.

Remind the group that the situations and people in the healing book or basket will benefit by the transmutational energies the circle generates. This same book or basket is used for each monthly circle. Energy is directed to these people, situations and places because the group intends this to be so, and because of the book's placement in the vortex center. As the healing energy envelopes and fills each person, it also radiates throughout the room and congeals in the center where the book is located at the circle's vortex. It travels up and out through the spiral from there. If using the basket, the papers from the participants can remain until the basket overflows. Then the facilitator can remove the papers and in private ceremony burn them, while connecting to the spirit of the earth, asking her to continue the healing begun when the each paper was placed in the basket.

During the hands-on work, insights may pop up for individuals related to the items in the basket or book. Also, emotions can bubble up during the healing segment, fresh angles glimpsed for tough personal issues and new perspectives gleaned for one's role in our rapidly changing world. In receiving healing energy people can more easily let go of past hurts and grievances to open their hearts. In doing so, they often gain a deeper understanding about their life's journey and what they may uniquely offer to the larger whole.

Support people in honoring these whisperings from spirit by asking them to write them down after the circle and ponder them at home. If what's been stirred for an individual demands some type of action on their part, this is best done in a manner and timing that feels right for them in order to elicit the universe's full participation. Actions can manifest as very personal and quiet life shifts, yet some are moved to impact visible social, environmental or political arenas. Remind folks that the universal life force is omnipresent, especially tangible through nature, and accessed through their open heart. They might want to drink a glass of water or have some food, mingle with people and share after the session and walk around before driving home. Yet again, it's good to stay heart-centered, not jumping into heady discussions.

**Sending Energy to Our Living World**
There are also other simple practices for group energy work. In the spring of 1999, Dream Change representatives buried Tibetan Buddhist Peace

Vases deep in the Amazon rainforest. In partnership with the Sacred Earth Network, a Peace Vase was also placed on the grounds of a Tibetan Buddhist temple in Kyzyl, Tuva. Another was buried by a river in the Shor Mountain region of Siberia. Initiated by His Holiness Dilgo Khyentse Rinpoche, hundreds of such vases were placed at points around the globe by volunteers. They contained consecrated items emanating blessings to the environment to avert negative occurrences and balance natural energies.

Many other indigenous groups, including the Maya, employ spiritual technology and ceremony to bring healing and blessings to the land, divert or balance potentially chaotic energies, and to harmonize human consciousness with the living earth. Most Shamanic Reiki practitioners can't follow their example by traveling the world in order to place their Reiki hands on the earth for healing and equilibrium. Yet they can live sustainably and in right relationship with her, encouraging others to do the same. They can also radiate blessings to the world by being clear and present, as well as actively sending energy to the earth and strengthening their connection with her.

Below is a Shamanic Reiki sending exercise adapted from a Tibetan practice. It can be used to send healing energy and compassion to any locale or situation on the earth, to shift our paradigm of separateness from the earth, as well as to ease existing and potential planetary conflict. This method is powerful in its ability to harmonize us with earth consciousness and highly effective for any group setting.

We do this practice in groups after spending conscious time in nature, doing ceremony or meditation together. It can also be done at the close of a *Community Healing Circle*. The group needs to be a harmonious vessel for life force energy. As a strong energy vortex naturally builds among people gathered with clear intention, the group should feel grounded, resonant and lucid, its energy potent.

Standing together in a circle and holding hands, we take three deep breaths, settling fully into our bodies and opening our hearts. In doing so, we feel the warmth of each other's hands and feel gratitude for each other and the earth that nurtures and sustains us. We feel our love for the earth, bringing to mind her exquisite beauty and allowing our appreciation for her to become a palpable force in our hearts. We breathe as one being in unison with earth and cosmic forces, immersed in the life force energy and feeling the loving intention of this energy. Reiki Level Two folks and above can invoke the Reiki symbols, individuals can also shapeshift into the Reiki energy or that of their Shamanic Reiki guides.

After the third breath releases, we focus on the Reiki energy spiral in the center of our circle. We take a few moments to feel the power of the vortex and may see, feel, intuit, hear or otherwise experience, the luminous and indestructible quality of this spiraling light. When the spiral is very real for us, we set our intention to offer energy wherever it's needed on our planet, wherever it's open to being received.

If desired, individuals can verbalize at this time some of the places or situations they intend for this energy to travel. For example: specific sites of environmental degradation, war and areas suffering from natural catastrophe, destructive political and social attitudes, world leaders, oil drilling sites in the rainforest and other environmental issues, future potential imbalances and chaos, or mindsets that separate us from nature. In speaking, and in hearing what others verbalize, we visualize or feel our connection to each situation. Each person firmly establishes himself or herself as a conduit of brilliant life force. Then each opens their heart to the confusion of the world, intending to emanate blessings, compassion, transmutation and balance through the vehicle of the universal life force. This can be a very emotional experience.

The designated leader of the group squeezes, and then gently releases, the hands he/she holds. Everyone in the circle does the same. Now, at the direction of the leader, people place their hands together in prayer position and, to focus and intensify the forces they will offer, rub their hands together rapidly (about 36 times). Heat radiates, concentration is alert, and heart and body are engaged. Each person prepares to offer out some of the merit, blessings and life force energy the group has magnetized.

On the count of the three everyone in the circle opens their hands with their palms facing upright, then camays (blows with the breath of spirit) through their palms toward the energy spiral, verbalizing a loud "shhhooo!" to propel the energy up and out of the room via the whirling vortex. As it does, people imagine, feel, see or simply know the energy is traveling to where it's needed. Arms rise up toward the sky, directing the healing forces to flow upward, out and beyond their circle. Some may intuit or see the scenes and circumstances receiving it. As the energy has its own intelligence, it will impact each situation uniquely, according to the highest good.

**Closing Inspiration**

Now it's your turn to discover the power of Reiki and shamanism. They are, by themselves, powerful ways to heal. Together, their power multiplies, and healing methods become available that aren't accessible if they're used separately. Our purpose in *Shamanic Reiki* has been to introduce you to concepts in both and provide you with detailed proven methods to enhance your own healing practices, or to work on yourselves. What we've presented here is not the end of knowledge about Shamanic Reiki, but the beginning. The particular beginning that's been illustrated throughout this book uniquely expresses the combined wisdom of each of our own approaches (the authors). As we did throughout these pages, we encourage you to utilize what we've presented in the way we do, or modify it to fit your needs and ways of healing. Shamanic Reiki is about cultivating your own relationship with spirit and intuiting the right collection of tools for each individual and circumstance.

Years of practice have shown us how potent a healing instrument Shamanic Reiki is. Through it, we learned long ago that miracles are ordinary, part of our human birthright. Practitioners facilitate the environment for each person to access their own wholeness in the timing and manner reflective of their highest good. In holding that space we've witnessed spontaneous physical healings that defy modern medical science. We've seen profound life changes. The work has shown us that each individual has the power to heal themselves, a power that's amplified in unconditional, loving environments. No one can predict the outcome of any session or healing relationship, yet in Shamanic Reiki we rest assured that whatever happens is meant to happen and we open to the unexpected. Our most important and exciting discovery is that the world is not, and we are not, as we've been conditioned to think. Embracing this practice has broadened our horizons and helped us relate to clients, ourselves, and the world from fresh perspectives. We see this expanded paradigm as essential for our own and our planet's health as we move together through increasingly complex times. We hope that you, who read this book, will also discover such powerful connections, enhancing your journey as a Shamanic Reiki healer and joining the universal circle of healers.

*May you always walk with spirit, may you benefit all who seek your help on their healing path and may these journeys benefit all of sentient life.*

# SELECTED BIBLIOGRAPHY

## MUSIC & JOURNEY CD'S

*Background for Journeys and Meditation* - Robert Y. Southard

*Drum Medicine* - David & Steve Gordon

*Environment Series* - Anugama

*Flowers in October* - Tim Janis

*HypnoJourney to the Amazon* - Robert Y. Southard

*Invoking the Muse* - Layne Redmond

*Mountains of Ice* - Angaangaq

*Pachacuti* - Alberto Taxo

*Pacific Grace; Spirit of the Killer Whale* - Dan Gibson's Solitudes

*Pan Flutes by the Ocean* - Ken Davis

*Pathways to Inner Peace* - Llyn Roberts & Robert Y. Southard

*Resonance of Ancestral Memories: The Healing Meditation* - Fabien Maman

*Reiki Whale Song* - Kamal

*Secrets of the Jungle* - Dan Gibson's Solitudes

*Shamanic Dream I & II* - Anugama

*Shamanic Healing* - Kamal

*Shamans Healing* - Shastro

*Tear of the Moon* - Coyote Oldman

*The Heart of Reiki* - Merlin's Magic

*Trust Your Inner Wisdom* - Nina Spiro


## BOOKS

*Empowerment through Reiki* - Paula Horan

*Essential Reiki* - Diane Stein

*Crystal Co Creators* - Dorothy Roeder

*Crystal Healing* - Katrina Raphael

*Healing with Form, Energy and Light* - Tenzin Wangyal, Rinpoche

*Listening to Nature* - Joseph Cornell

*Medicine for the Earth* - Sandra Ingerman

*Old Souls* - Tom Shroeder

*Ordinary Secrets; Notes for Your Spiritual Journey* - Robert Y. Southard

*Reiki Magick* - Christopher Penczak

*Reiki, The Healing Touch: First and Second Degree Manual* - William Lee Rand

*Sacred World* - Jeremy & Karen Hayward

*Shamanism as a Spiritual Practice for Daily Life* - Tom Cowan

*Shapeshifting; Techniques for Global and Personal Transformation* - John Perkins

*Soul Retrieval: Mending the Fragmented Self* - Sandra Ingerman

*The Celtic Shaman: A Handbook* - John Matthews

*The Good Remembering; A Message for Our Times* - Llyn Roberts

*The Healing Power of Mind* - Tulku Thondup

*The Secret Life of Plants* - Peter Tompkins & Christopher Bird

*The Shamans Body* - Arnold Mindell

*The Twelve Stages of Healing* - Donald M. Epstein, D.C.

*The World Is As You Dream It* - John Perkins

*Way of the Shaman* - Michael Harner

*Welcome Home; Following Your Soul's Journey Home* - Sandra Ingerman

*When the Drummers Were Women* - Layne Redmond

# ABOUT THE AUTHORS

*Llyn Roberts* has practiced Usui Reiki from early 1989, taught non-traditional Reiki since 1993 and Shamanic Reiki since 1996. She holds a master's degree in Tibetan Buddhist and Western Psychology from Naropa University and was a student of Chogyam Trungpa, Rinpoche. Llyn has designed and led trips to work with shamans and elders living in remote regions of the Amazon basin, the Asian steppes, high Andes, and in ancient lands of Central America's Maya. She has undergone extensive training with traditional Quechua peoples and is an initiate of birdpeople shamanic circles in Siberia and Ecuador. Llyn is also trained in western psychic healing and body-mind modalities, has directed programs and teaches at the Omega Institute and other educational institutions in the US and Europe, and directed the non-profit organization, Dream Change (applying indigenous wisdom for personal and global change). She wrote *The Good Remembering; A Message for Our Times* (O-Books). To learn more about Llyn Roberts and her work: llynroberts.com

*Robert Levy* originally trained in the Usui Reiki tradition. He has been a non-traditional Reiki master practitioner and teacher, as well as a shamanic practitioner, since 1995. Robert combines, and encourages his students to combine, other healing modalities with Reiki. He has separately assisted John Perkins, Llyn Roberts and Dr Eve Bruce in shamanic workshops at the Omega Institute for many years and worked alongside them and indigenous shamanic teachers at Dream Change's *Gathering of Shamans/Wisdom Keepers* at Omega. Robert has studied with western shamans as well as those from Brazil, Peru and Ecuador. His primary teachers are Ipupiara Makunaiman from the Ure-e-wau-wau tribe of Brazil and Peruvian-born, Cleicha Toscano. Robert Levy lives and practices Shamanic Reiki in NYC. He is Dream Change's *WOW! Community Program (WCP!)* regional groups coordinator: www.dreamchange. org or ShamanicReiki@aol.com

Llyn Roberts and Robert Levy will respond to enquiries about private work, public appearances and further study in Shamanic Reiki, but high volume may make it impossible to answer all emails regarding the opinions and reactions to this book.

# BOOKS

O is a symbol of the world, of oneness and unity. In different cultures it also means the "eye," symbolizing knowledge and insight. We aim to publish books that are accessible, constructive and that challenge accepted opinion, both that of academia and the "moral majority."

Our books are available in all good English language bookstores worldwide. If you don't see the book on the shelves ask the bookstore to order it for you, quoting the ISBN number and title. Alternatively you can order online (all major online retail sites carry our titles) or contact the distributor in the relevant country, listed on the copyright page.

See our website www.o-books.net for a full list of over 500 titles, growing by 100 a year.

And tune in to myspiritradio.com for our book review radio show, hosted by June-Elleni Laine, where you can listen to the authors discussing their books.

MySpiritRadio

## The Good Remembering
**Llyn Roberts**

*I stumbled into The Good Remembering and felt compelled to read it from cover to cover. Now I recommend it to anyone searching for insight into spiritual growth during these intense times. Responsibly and well-written, it is a magical, powerful little book that transcends words and speaks directly to soul.* **Melody Beattie**, New York Times Best Selling author of *Co-Dependent No More*
1846940389 96pp £7.99 $16.95

## Back to the Truth
**5,000 years of Advaita**
**Dennis Waite**

*A wonderful book. Encyclopedic in nature, and destined to become a classic.* **James Braha**
*Absolutely brilliant...an ease of writing with a water-tight argument outlining the great universal truths. This book will become a modern classic. A milestone in the history of Advaita.* **Paula Marvelly**
1905047614 500pp £19.95 $29.95

## Beyond Photography
**Encounters with orbs, angels and mysterious light forms**
**Katie Hall and John Pickering**

*The authors invite you to join them on a fascinating quest; a voyage of discovery into the nature of a phenomenon, manifestations of which are shown as being historical and global as well as contemporary and intently personal.*
*At journey's end you may find yourself a believer, a doubter or simply*

*an intrigued wonderer... Whatever the outcome, the process of journeying is likely prove provocative and stimulating and - as with the mysterious images fleetingly captured by the authors' cameras - inspiring and potentially enlightening.* **Brian Sibley**, author and broadcaster.
1905047908 272pp 50 b/w photos +8pp colour insert **£12.99 $24.95**

## Don't Get MAD Get Wise
**Why no one ever makes you angry, ever!**
**Mike George**

There is a journey we all need to make, from anger, to peace, to forgiveness. Anger always destroys, peace always restores, and forgiveness always heals. This explains the journey, the steps you can take to make it happen for you.
1905047827 160pp **£7.99 $14.95**

## IF You Fall...
**It's a new beginning**
**Karen Darke**

*Karen Darke's story is about the indomitability of spirit, from one of life's cruel vagaries of fortune to what is insight and inspiration. She has overcome the limitations of paralysis and discovered a life of challenge and adventure that many of us only dream about. It is all about the mind, the spirit and the desire that some of us find, but which all of us possess.* **Joe Simpson**, mountaineer and author of *Touching the Void*
1905047886 240pp £9.99 $19.95

## Love, Healing and Happiness
**Spiritual wisdom for a post-secular era**
**Larry Culliford**

*This will become a classic book on spirituality. It is immensely practical and grounded. It mirrors the author's compassion and lays the foundation*

*for a higher understanding of human suffering and hope.* **Reinhard Kowalski** Consultant Clinical Psychologist
1905047916 304pp **£10.99 $19.95**


## A Map to God
**Awakening Spiritual Integrity**
**Susie Anthony**

This describes an ancient hermetic pathway, representing a golden thread running through many traditions, which offers all we need to understand and do to actually become our best selves.
1846940443 260pp **£10.99 $21.95**


## Punk Science
Inside the mind of God
Manjir Samanta-Laughton

*Wow! Punk Science is an extraordinary journey from the microcosm of the atom to the macrocosm of the Universe and all stops in between. Manjir Samanta-Laughton's synthesis of cosmology and consciousness is sheer genius. It is elegant, simple and, as an added bonus, makes great reading.* **Dr Bruce H. Lipton**, author of *The Biology of Belief*
1905047932 320pp **£12.95 $22.95**


## Rosslyn Revealed
**A secret library in stone**
**Alan Butler**

Rosslyn Revealed gets to the bottom of the mystery of the chapel featured in the Da Vinci Code. The results of a lifetime of careful research and study demonstrate that truth really is stranger than fiction; a library of philo-sophical ideas and mystery rites, that were heresy in their time, have been disguised in the extraordinarily elaborate stone carvings.
1905047924 260pp b/w + colour illustrations **£19.95 $29.95** cl

## The Way of Thomas
**Nine Insights for Enlightened Living from the Secret Sayings of Jesus**
**John R. Mabry**

What is the real story of early Christianity? Can we find a Jesus that is relevant as a spiritual guide for people today?

These and many other questions are addressed in this popular presentation of the teachings of this mystical Christian text. Includes a reader-friendly version of the gospel.
1846940303 196pp **£10.99 $19.95**

## The Way Things Are
**A Living Approach to Buddhism**
**Lama Ole Nydahl**

An up-to-date and revised edition of a seminal work in the Diamond Way Buddhist tradition (three times the original length), that makes the timeless wisdom of Buddhism accessible to western audiences. Lama Ole has established more than 450 centres in 43 countries.
1846940427 240pp **£9.99 $19.95**

## A-Z of Reiki Pocketbook
**Everything About Reiki**
**Bronwen and Frans Stiene**

*A-Z of Reiki, the latest work by Bronwen and Frans Stiene, is an all-encompassing and expansive glossary of Reiki and Japanese healing. This book helps clear the way for everyone to partake of Reiki.* **Nina Paul**, author of *Reiki for Dummies*
1905047894 272pp 125/90mm **£7.99 $16.95**

# Energy Works!
## Initiation without a master
## Teresa Parrott and Graham Crook

*Graham and Teresa have explored the world of SKHM to a depth that few have been able to achieve, and, most importantly, they have been able to share their experience with others through their words in the most beautiful way. Those who read about their experience will be initiated in a journey of the heart. I highly recommend allowing yourself to experience that journey.* **Patrick Zeigler**
1905047525 304pp **£12.99 $24.95**


# Healing Hands
## Simple and practical reflexology techniques for developing god health and inner peace
## David Vennells

*Promising good health and inner peace, this practical guide to reflexology techniques may not be a glossy affair but it is thoroughly and clearly illustrated. Hand reflexology isn't as well known as the foot variety, but it's undeniably effective and, perhaps most usefully, it's a technique that can be applied for self-treatment. Whatever the healing process is that you're going through, whenever you're experiencing it, Healing Hands can support your journey.* **Wave**
1905047126 192pp **£9.99 $16.95**


# The Japanese Art of Reiki
## A practical guide to self healing
## Bronwen and Frans Stiene

2nd printing
*This is a sequel to the aclaimed "Reiki Sourcebook." For those of us in the West who see adverts for weekend Reiki Master courses and wonder about the authenticity of the tradition, this book is an eye-opener. It takes the*

*reader back to the Japanese roots of the tradition in a way that conveys its inspirational power and cultural flavour. The book is illustrated and is full of practical guidance for both practitioners and general readers.* **Scientific and Medical Network Review**
1905047029 208pp **£12.99 $19.95**

## Reiki Jin Kei Do
**The way of compassion and wisdom**
**Steve Gooch**

*Steve Gooch has done an excellent job in presenting to the public the world's first book on the deeply profound and beautiful teachings that were given to me by Seiji Takamori. In doing so he has become the spokesperson for the whole lineage. I recommend it highly to all.* **Dr Ranga Premaratna**, Lineage Head of Reiki Jin Kei Do
1905047851 240pp **£12.99 $21.95**

## Reiki Mastery
**For second degree students and masters**
**David Vennells**

3rd printing
*A compassionate, wise, handbook to making the most of the Life Force Energy that surrounds and informs us all.*
*An excellent reference for anyone interested in hands-on healing. Helpful and insightful, good and solid.* Amazon
190381670X 192pp **£9.99 $14.95**

## Reiki Q&A: 200 Questions & Answers for Beginners
**Lawrence Ellyard**

2nd printing
*This unique handbook clearly answers all kinds of questions about Reiki and its practice as well as dispelling any misconceptions. Useful,*

*dependable and highly recommended.* **Penny Parkes**, author of *15-minute Reiki*
1905047479 208pp **£12.99 $24.95**

## Reiki Techniques Card Deck
### Heal Yourself Intuitively
**Bronwen and Frans Stiene**

Everyone has the ability to initiate self-healing-it is your birthright. The techniques in this deck of 45 cards, selected from the most effective traditional and non-traditional Reiki techniques from around the globe, offer you the opportunity to consciously tap into your healing ability, supporting you on your natural path.
1905047193 24pp + 40 colour cards, box 88/127mm **£15.99 $24.95**

## Ultimate Reiki Guide for Practitioners and Masters
**Lawrence Ellyard**

2nd printing
*In this excellent volume, Lawrence Ellyard brings together his considerable expertise and experience to provide a clear and concise view of how to conduct Reiki and to establish oneself as a Reiki practitioner. It will be invaluable for all Reiki professionals and lay persons as a spiritual, practice and business guide.* **Dr. Ralph Locke**, CEO, Ikon
1905047487 208pp **£12.99 $24.95**

## Your Reiki Treatment
**Bronwen and Frans Stiene**

This is the first title to look at Reiki from the client's perspective. Whether you are searching for relaxation, healing, or spiritual growth, a Reiki treatment can be a revelation. Find out how to make the most of it. Learn how to prepare, what to expect, and how to continue furthering your personal growth after the treatment is finished.

18469490133 240pp **£9.99 $19.95**

## Colours of the Soul
**Transform your life through colour therapy**
**June McLeod**

*A great book, the best I've read on the subject and so inspirational.* **Laura**, Helios Centre

*One of those books that makes a deep and lasting impression on our lives.* **Chrissy Wright**
1905047258 176pp + 4pp colour insert **£11.99 $21.95**

## Crystal Prescriptions
**The A-Z guide to over 1,200 symptoms and their healing crystals**
**Judy Hall**

2nd printing
*Another potential best-seller. This handy little book is packed as tight as a pill-bottle with crystal remedies for ailments. It is written in an easy-to-understand style, so if you are not a virtuoso with your Vanadinite, it will guide you. If you love crystals and want to make the best use of them, invest in this book as a complete reference to their healing qualities.* **Vision**
1905047401 176pp 2 colour **£7.99 $15.95**

## Grow Youthful
**A practical guide to slowing your ageing**
**David Niven Miller**

Over the millennia, many extraordinary people have lived well beyond a century. This easy to understand book reveals many of the secrets. Supported by recent scientific research, it cuts through much of the jargon and conflict concerning health and longevity.
1846940044 224pp **£10.00 $19.95**

## The Healing Power of Celtic Plants
**Healing herbs of the ancient Celts and their Druid medicine men**
**Angela Paine**

Each plant is covered here in depth, explaining its history, myth and symbolism and also how to grow, preserve, prepare and use them. Uniquely, here, their properties are examined together with the scientific evidence that they work.
1905047622 304pp 250/153mm b/w illustrations **£16.99 $29.95**

## The Healing Sourcebook
**Learn to heal yourself and others**
**David Vennells**

Here is the distilled wisdom of many years practice; a number of complementary therapies which are safe, easy to learn from a book, and combine wonderfully with each other to form a simple but powerful system of healing for body and mind.
1846940052 320pp **£14.99 $22.95**

## Healing the Eternal Soul
**Insights from past life and spiritual regression**
**Andy Tomlinson**

*Written with simple precision and sprinkled with ample case examples this will be an invaluable resource for those who assist others in achieving contact with the eternal part of themselves. It is an invaluable contribution and advancement to the field of Regression Therapy. More so, it is an incredibly interesting read!* **Dr. Arthur E. Roffey**, Past Vice-President, Society for Spiritual Regression
190504741X 288pp **£14.99 $29.95**

## Humming Your Way to Happiness

**An introduction to Tuva and overtone singing from around the world**
**Peter Galgut**

*An engaging tour of the field by a medical scientist that takes the reader into the cross-cultural landscape of sound, with special emphasis on Tuva and overtone singing. The author puts his journey into a wide context so that the reader can understand the role that sounds have played in various parts of the world, and also considers sounds, music and religions as well as the use of sound therapy.* **Scientific and Medical Network Review**
1905047142 144pp **£9.99 $19.95**

## The Invisible Disease

**The dangers of environmental illnesses caused by electromagnetic fields and chemical emissions**
**Gunni Nordstrom**

*Highly recommended. This most informative and well written book makes the connections between the ranges of illnesses and chemicals used in the manufacture of modern appliances that are mistakenly considered safe. They are not.* **Luminous Times**
1903816718 256pp **£9.99 $14.95**

## Masters of Health

**The original sources of today's alternative therapies**
**Robert van de Weyer**

More and more people have been turning to alternative approaches to health and illness, especially those that have been tried and tested over many centuries. Here are the major original texts, from eastern and western traditions, rendered into modern idiom. With introductions to each, they form a summary of ancient wisdom on human wholeness.
1905047150 192pp **£9.99 $19.95**

## The Theorem
### A complete answer to human behaviour
### Douglas Arone

*Arguably the genius of any great discovery lies in its originality-a fresh idea that is set to challenge traditional modes of thinking while advancing man's march along the path of progress. Far from the idea that the human foetus is cocooned from the cares and woes of existence, our first experience of fear, joy and sorrow actually precedes our birth. This in a nutshell is what this book is set to tell the world. (The author) has accomplished his task with exceptional brilliance.* **B. K. Abolade** MD; MRCP (UK), Child and Adolescent Psychiatrist, Alabama
190504710X 496pp **£19.99 $39.95**

## Universal Principles and the Metamorphic Technique
### The keys to healing and enlightenment
### Gaston St-Pierre

*It has slowly and quietly gained respect from not only those whose lives have been transformed by it, but from doctors and specialists impressed with the results for conditions ranging from doctors and specialists impressed with the results for conditions ranging from dyslexia to eating disorders.* **Lorna V**. *The Sunday Times*
    *Thousands who have experienced the technique affirm that life is never the same once you step onto the metamorphic path.* **Jane Alexander**, **Daily Mail**
1903816602 308pp **£11.99 $19.95**

## Daughters of the Earth
### Cheryl Straffon

*Combines legend, landscape and women's ceremonies to create a wonderful mixture of Goddess experience in the present day. A feast of information, ideas, facts and visions.* **Kathy Jones**, co-founder of the

Glastonbury Goddess Conference
1846940168 240pp **£11.99 $21.95**


## The Gods Within
**An interactive guide to archetypal therapy**
**Peter Lemesurier**

*Whether you enjoy analyzing your family and friends or looking for ways
to explain or excuse your own strengths and weaknesses, this book provides
a whole new slant. It can be read just for fun, but there is an uncanny ring
of truth to it. Peter Lemesurier combines scholarship with wry humour, a
compulsive mixture.* **Anna Corser**, Physiotherapy Manager
1905047991 416pp **£14.99 $29.95**


## Maiden, Mother, Crone
**Voices of the Goddess**
**Claire Hamilton**

*This is a vividly written and evocative series of stories in which Celtic
goddesses speak in the first person about their lives and experiences. It
enables the reader to reconnect with a neglected but resurgent tradition
that is a part of the advent of the feminine in our time.* **Scientific and
Medical Network Review**
1905047398 240pp **£12.99 $24.95**


## The Sacred Wheel of the Year
**Tess Ward**

*A spiritual handbook full of wisdom, grace and creativity. It dips into the
deep wells of Celtic tradition and beyond to gather the clear water of life.
This is a book of prayer to be treasured.* **Mike Riddell**, author of *The
Sacred Journey*
1905047959 260pp **£11.99 $24.95**

## Savage Breast
### One man's search for the goddess
### Tim Ward

*An epic, elegant, scholarly search for the goddess, weaving together travel, Greek mythology, and personal autobiographic relationships into a remarkable exploration of the Western World's culture and sexual history. It is also entertainingly human, as we listen and learn from this accomplished person and the challenging mate he wooed. If you ever travel to Greece, take Savage Breast along with you.* **Harold Schulman**, Professor of Gynaecology at Winthrop University Hospital, and author of *An Intimate History of the Vagina.*
1905047584 400pp colour section +100 b/w photos **£12.99 $19.95**

## Tales of the Celtic Bards
### With CD
### Claire Hamilton

*An original and compelling retelling of some wonderful stories by an accomplished mistress of the bardic art. Unusual and refreshing, the book provides within its covers the variety and colour of a complete bardic festival.* **Ronald Hutton**, Professor of History

*Harp music perfectly complements the book in a most haunting way. A perfect way in to the tales of "the Strange Ones".* **Wave**
1903816548 320pp with CD 230/152mm **£16.99 $24.95** cl.